Death and (Re)Birth of J. S. Bach

While the study and redefinition of the notion of authorship and its relationship to the idea of the literary work have played a central role in recent research on literature, semiotics, and related disciplines, its impact on contemporary musicology is still limited. Why? What implications would a reconsideration of the author- and work-concepts have on our understanding of the creative musical processes? Why would such a reexamination of these regulative concepts be necessary? Could it emerge from a post-structuralist revision of the notion of musical textuality? In this book, Trillo takes the . . . *Bach* . . . project, a collection of new music based on Johann Sebastian Bach's Partita No.1 for solo violin, BWV 1002, as a point of departure to sketch some critical answers to these fundamental questions, raise new ones, and explore their musicological implications.

Dr Roberto Alonso Trillo was born in Vigo (Spain) in 1983. His professional career ranges over three interrelated areas: performance, pedagogy, and research. As a violin player, he has developed an active international performing career, accentuating his performance with academic investigations of authorship, audience, and creativity. At present, Dr Trillo works as a visiting lecturer at different international institutions in Europe and America. Examples of recent research have been published by the *Perspectives of New Music* magazine, *Hispanic Research Journal*, and the *IRASM* magazine. His areas of specialization include twentieth-century music and contemporary Spanish music, a wide interest in Theodor W. Adorno's sociology and philosophy of music, the history of violin teaching and performance, performance analysis with digital tools, and a general music-based interest in the work and ideas of French post-structuralist thinkers. For further info, please visit www.robertoalonsotrillo.com.

Death and (Re)Birth of J. S. Bach

Reconsidering Musical Authorship and the Work-Concept

Roberto Alonso Trillo

LONDON AND NEW YORK

First published 2019 by Routledge

2 Park Square, Milton Park, Abingdon, Oxon, OX14 4RN
605 Third Avenue, New York, NY 10017

Routledge is an imprint of the Taylor & Francis Group, an informa business

First issued in paperback 2020

British Library Cataloguing-in-Publication Data
A catalogue record for this book is available from the British Library

Library of Congress Cataloging-in-Publication Data
Names: Trillo, Roberto Alonso, 1983– author.
Title: Death and (re)birth of J.S. Bach: reconsidering authorship and the musical work/ Roberto Alonso Trillo.
Description: Abingdon, Oxon ; New York, NY : Routledge, 2019. | Includes bibliographical references and index.
Identifiers: LCCN 2018042999 | ISBN 9781138586260 (hardback) | ISBN 9780429504716 (ebook)
Subjects: LCSH: Bach, Johann Sebastian, 1685–1750—Criticism and interpretation. | Authorship—Philosophy.
Classification: LCC ML410.B13 T73 2019 | DDC 780.92—dc23
LC record available at https://lccn.loc.gov/2018042999

ISBN: 978-1-138-58626-0 (hbk)
ISBN: 978-0-367-73255-4 (pbk)

Typeset in Times New Roman
by Apex CoVantage, LLC

For Ana, Aaminah, and Daniel

Contents

Illustrations and audiovisual material

Examples

Tables

Figures

Charts

Videos

The audio examples can be accessed via the online Routledge Music Research Portal: www.routledgemusicresearch.co.uk. Please enter the activation word **RRMusic** and your e-mail address when prompted. You will immediately be sent an automated e-mail containing an access token and instructions, which will allow you to log onto the site.

Pre-text

On May 9, 1992, the British daily newspaper *The Times* published the following letter:

> Sir, The University of Cambridge is to ballot on May 16 on whether M. Jacques Derrida should be allowed to go forward to receive an honorary degree. As philosophers and others who have taken a scholarly and professional interest in M. Derrida's remarkable career over the years, we believe the following might throw some needed light on the public debate that has arisen over this issue.
>
> Derrida describes himself as a philosopher, and his writings do indeed bear some of the marks of writings in that discipline. Their influence, however, has been to a striking degree almost entirely in fields outside philosophy – in departments of film studies, for example, or of French and English literature.
>
> In the eyes of philosophers, and certainly among those working in leading departments of philosophy throughout the world, M. Derrida's work does not meet accepted standards of clarity and rigour. We submit that, if the works of a physicist (say) were similarly taken to be of merit primarily by those working in other disciplines, this would in itself be sufficient grounds for casting doubt upon the idea that the physicist in question was a suitable candidate for an honorary degree.
>
> Derrida's career had its roots in the heady days of the 1960s and his writings continue to reveal their origins in that period. Many of them seem to consist in no small part of elaborate jokes and puns ("logical phallusies" and the like), and M. Derrida seems to us to have come close to making a career out of what we regard as translating into the academic sphere tricks and gimmicks similar to those of the Dadaists or of the concrete poets.
>
> Certainly he has shown considerable originality in this respect. But again, we submit, such originality does not lend credence to the idea that he is a suitable candidate for an honorary degree. Many French

> philosophers see in M. Derrida only cause for silent embarrassment, his antics having contributed significantly to the widespread impression that contemporary French philosophy is little more than an object of ridicule.
>
> Derrida's voluminous writings in our view stretch the normal forms of academic scholarship beyond recognition. Above all – as every reader can very easily establish for himself (and for this purpose any page will do) – his works employ a written style that defies comprehension.
>
> Many have been willing to give M. Derrida the benefit of the doubt, insisting that language of such depth and difficulty of interpretation must hide deep and subtle thoughts indeed.
>
> When the effort is made to penetrate it, however, it becomes clear, to us at least, that, where coherent assertions are being made at all, these are either false or trivial.
>
> Academic status based on what seems to us to be little more than semi-intelligible attacks upon the values of reason, truth, and scholarship is not, we submit, sufficient grounds for the awarding of an honorary degree in a distinguished university.
>
> (Smith 1992)

A few years ago, almost a decade after the publication of Barry Smith's letter, I first had contact with the Derridean universe through a book entitled *Ghostly Demarcations: A Symposium on Jacques Derrida's Specters of Marx* (Sprinker 1999). I was impressed by the controversy surrounding the French thinker's ideas, especially by Terry Eagleton's critical approach, and decided to embark on my own reading and revision of Derrida's work.

On the occasion of Derrida's death, on October 15, 2004, Eagleton wrote the following words in the British journal *The Guardian*:

> English philistinism continues to flourish, not least when the words "French philosopher" are uttered. This week in the Guardian our home-grown intelligentsia gave a set of bemused, bone-headed responses to the death of Jacques Derrida. Either they hadn't read him, or they believed his work was to do with words not meaning what you think they do. Or it was just a pile of garbage.
>
> In line with this judicious assessment, Derrida – one of the most eminent postwar French thinkers – was turned down for an honorary degree at Cambridge University. The man was regarded by the stuffed shirts as a subversive nihilist who believed that words could mean anything you liked, that truth was a fiction, and that there was nothing in the world but writing. In their eyes, he was a dangerous mixture of anarchist, poet and jester.
>
> But the dons who voted him down were the kind of scrupulous academics who had almost certainly not read his books. They knew he

> was radical, enigmatic, French, photogenic and wildly popular with students. The university had the good sense to reverse its decision later; but many academics regard him as a man out to destroy philosophy, thus depriving some of them of a living.
>
> In fact, Derrida rejoiced in the pantheon of philosophy from Plato to Heidegger. Deconstruction, the philosophical method he promoted, means not destroying ideas, but pushing them to the point where they begin to come apart and expose their latent contradictions. It meant reading against the grain of supposedly self-evident truths, rather than taking them for granted. English senior common rooms are full of self-righteous blather about thinkers like Derrida being more interested in abstract theories than in close reading. In fact, he read works of art and philosophy with a stunning originality and intricacy beyond that of most of his critics. (Eagleton 2004)

In 2013, the Spanish cartoonist Andrés Rábago García "El Roto" included the drawing shown in Example 0.1, which can be seen as a satiric depiction

Example 0.1 A. R. García, *Oh, la l'art!, The Academia*

of the resistance to Derrida's ideas, in a book entitled *Oh, la l'art!* (Rábago García 2013).

Twenty-five years after the publication of Smith's letter of objection to the granting of an honorary degree by the University of Cambridge, eighteen years after the publication of *Ghostly Demarcations: A Symposium on Jacques Derrida,* and thirteen years after the death of the French thinker, many scholars would argue that the significance and the apparent threat posed by his work and ideas have diminished, if not vanished. Is that the case? This book is my own reply to this absurdly beautiful controversy, a daring reopening of a critical conversation to which I was never invited but one that I take as a gift and happily enter as an outsider.

References

Eagleton, Terry. "Don't Deride Derrida." *The Guardian*, October 15, 2004, accessed February 23, 2018, www.theguardian.com/education/2004/oct/15/highereducation.news

Rábago García, Andrés. *Oh, la l'art!* Barcelona: Editorial el Zorro Rojo, 2013.

Smith, Barry, et al. *The Times*, May 9, 1992, accessed February 23, 2018, http://ontology.buffalo.edu/smith/varia/Derrida_Letter.htm

Sprinker, Michael, ed. *Ghostly Demarcations: A Symposium on Jacques Derrida's Specters of Marx*. New York: Verso, 2008.

Introduction

> Central to the historical thesis is the claim that Bach did not intend to compose musical works. Only by adopting a modern perspective – a perspective foreign to Bach – would we say that he had . . . [T]he concepts governing musical practice before 1800 precluded the regulative function of the work-concept.
>
> (Goehr 2007: 8)

While the study and redefinition of the notion of authorship and its relationship to the idea of the literary work has played a central role in recent research on literature, semiotics, and related disciplines, its impact on contemporary musicology is still limited. Why? What implications would a reconsideration of the dominant work- and author-concepts have on our understanding of the creative musical processes?[1] Why would such a reexamination of these regulative concepts be necessary? Could it emerge from a post-structuralist revision of the notion of musical textuality? In this book, I take the . . . *Bach* . . . project, a collection of new music based on Johann Sebastian Bach's Partita No.1 for solo violin BWV 1002, as a point of departure to sketch some critical answers to these fundamental questions, raise new ones, and explore their musicological implications.[2] But why Bach's BWV 1002?

Bach's Partita No. 1 exemplifies what Kenneth Lutterman defines as "artifacts of improvisatory practices" (Lutterman 2006: 8). The Partita presents a set of four movement-pairs comprised of four main dance-related sections – Allemanda, Corrente, Sarabande, and Tempo di Borea – and their respective *doubles*. Bach's seemingly improvisatory *doubles*, through their combination of an ornamental re-elaboration of the figured bass progression of the preceding dance-inspired music and an exploration of the variation technique of diminution (a division of longer note values into shorter melodic ones), offer a path of performative and compositional continuation.

The . . . *Bach* . . . project follows this open path to introduce a contemporary expansion of Bach's original, one that stems from Lutterman's conception. As such, it provides the necessary material to draft a reconsideration of the work-concept and of musical authorship, a revision based here on a selective reading of Roland Barthes's authorial theories and on a critical adaptation of specific aspects of Jacques Derrida's intellectuality.

The . . . *Bach* . . . project emerges from an understanding of Bach's musical creation as performance- rather than production- or work-concept-based. I argue that music in the Baroque period was still a predominantly performance-focused activity; it was event centered and not an abstract score-based one, not an essentially reified abstraction. Previous research has linked the rise of the modern work-concept to the primarily product-focused understanding of music that became prevalent in the mid- to late eighteenth century (Goehr 2007: 253). From that perspective, Bach's author-relationship with the BWV 1002 might be at odds with, and hence should not be filtered through, the influential *opus perfectum* ideal or the Romantic Goethian notion of *letzter hand*.[3] Lydia Goehr points out that such approaches are a case of "conceptual imperialism," a rewriting of music history that started "around 1800 when musicians began to reconstruct musical history to make it look as if musicians had always thought about their activities in modern terms" (Goehr 2007: 245).[4] The shift of the moment of completion from the text/score back to its performance makes possible an understanding of Bach's music as a work-in-progress. While providing the original set of dances and introducing a first elaboration, the German composer's BWV 1002 institutes a pattern open to potential continuation. The . . . *Bach* . . . project was therefore conceived as a furthering of Bach's opening gesture: twelve new *doubles* were written by an international selection of living composers to refresh and transform the original material. These expansions become a contemporary reflection on a creative gesture initiated almost three hundred years ago. The . . . *Bach* . . . project consequently challenges the closedness of Bach's Partita: are these new *doubles* to be considered as an extraneous addendum, or do they become part of, expand, or parasite Bach's compositional gesture? Can music parallel Barthes's definition of literature as a "composite, oblique space where our subject slips away, the negative where all identity is lost, starting with the very identity of the body writing"? (Barthes 1977: 142). Can the opposition between *original* and *derived* material lose its pertinence, following Derrida's reading, "from the moment we recognize that everything begins by following a vestige or trace, i.e. a certain repetition or textuality" (Cobussen 2002: 99)? This book opens with a consideration of the poiesis of the . . . *Bach* . . . project. The first chapter explores the inspirational example provided by the filmic correspondences initiated by Victor Erice and Abbas Kiarostami, through a proposal of the Barcelona Centre for Contemporary Culture, and subsequently expanded by five further pairs of film directors (Erice and Kiarostami 2006). I analyze how these filmic exchanges were conceived as a questioning of some of the dominant ideas that permeate most contemporary authorship theories. The following section explores how the . . . *Bach* . . . project reflected those elements. Finally, a brief remark on the nature of the project's commissions leads to the introduction of the three fundamental questions – presented as three challenges to "traditional musicology" – that this text attempts to answer.

Chapter 2 considers the development of authorship theories in the field of literary criticism during the second half of the twentieth century. These are used as an intellectual background to explore, from a historicist perspective, the emergence of the modern musical work- and author-concepts and their contemporary revisions. Have these new readings met the intellectual challenges introduced by the advancement of authorship theories in the literary field? Would such a parallelism be necessary or constructive? And, if that is the case, what remains to be done? Chapter 3 explores how some of the intellectual gestures found in the writings of Barthes and Derrida might be used to this end. I thus present a brief discussion of Barthesian authoriality and of the analytical meaning and bearing of some key Derridean *lexemes* such as *dissémination*, *signature*, *différance*, *archi-écriture*, and *trace*. These notions help us sketch a first tentative answer to the key questions introduced at the end of Chapter 1. But how can these ideas bear an impact on a musical-analytical perspective?

Chapter 4 introduces a model based on an analytical framework that explores some of the "markers" that reveal Bach's authorship of the Partita. "Authorship markers" are conceived as elements that disclose the traces of Bach's compositional gestures, including the work's overall formal conception, the stylized nature of the dances and the *doubles*, their harmonic structure, the exploration of idiomatic writing, Bach's music as a reflection of a sounding space, and the gestural dimension of the German's music.[5] These markers are embedded in and emerge from Bach's own conception of music and originality.[6] My analysis thus connects, from this unique analytical perspective, Bach's music to four contemporary expansions of the Partita's structure taken from the . . . *Bach* . . . project: the new *doubles* composed by Fernando Buide, Miguel Matamoro, Tomás Marco, and Esaias Järnegard. I analyze each case study separately, applying the intellectual framework developed in the earlier consideration of Barthesian and Derridean thinking. My research presents these specific re-elaborations of Bach's music as examples that question the dominant work- and author-concepts and put forward new definitions tangentially linked to other significant theoretical notions such as Adorno's conception of "musical material"[7] – a vision of musical material as historically mediated – and Hepokoski and Darcy's discussion of "dialogic form" – an understanding of musical form as processual and a vision of the composer's work as "a dialogue with an intricate web of interrelated norms" (Hepokoski and Darcy 2006: 10).[8] The newly emerging notions take into account similar discussions in the fields of literary criticism and philosophy but remain idiosyncratically musicological.

Let me point out, before we embark on the ensuing musicological journey, that the reader should not expect to find here a well-defined methodology but a mere philosophy of interpretation. My arguments have been openly conceived and structured in a non-methodological manner. As such, they are permeated by a certain sense of circularity and cannot be reduced to a replicable analytical pattern, a dry formula. They introduce instead an analytical framework, an intellectual apparatus, that might be used elsewhere only if subjected to further modifications. Do the analytical patterns emerge from the material under examination, or am I imposing my preformed ideas on the material? How should I face the inescapability of the hermeneutic circle? Am I not condemned to stand at an in-between position? Even if it is undeniable that Barthes's and Derrida's work and ideas have had a clear influence on my thinking, it is also true that my reflections depart from a purely musicological and performative consideration of the . . . *Bach* . . . project and the example provided by the filmic correspondences. I am not attempting to define specific notions of authorship or workhood that might be adequately applied to a study of J. S. Bach's music. Bach is an example, an excuse, an enlightening case study, but my reflection is and remains global, engaging in a much wider discussion of key musicological concepts. I am trying to reconsider those concepts beyond the historicist reassessment, exploring the implications of musical authorship from a novel perspective, analyzing the material that authors work with, their relationship to it, and examining the fundamental roles of performance and reception. The text openly accepts that it is "alien" to Bach's case (or to any other specific case) to the same extent that any intellectualization remains necessarily "alien" to the intellectualized activity. What I am questioning here is the nature of the alienation and the necessity to continuously reconsider it. The strength of my proposal is its weakness; it lives in that paradox, in the self-awareness of the power of its fleetingness. Furthermore, my discussions are not end oriented, they do not attempt to present truisms as conclusive gestures, but are process oriented, focusing instead on the nature of the critical reflective mechanisms. As a result, my overall arguments should not – and cannot – be subjected to value (right/wrong) judgments since they simply aim to demonstrate not only that thinking differently is possible but that it might lead us to an understanding of music that remains more truthful, more closely connected to its nature as a multifaceted and transdisciplinary activity.

Notes

1 These dominant concepts can be related to what David Davies defines as the "classical paradigm," according to which:

> performances are *of* performable works and play a necessary part in their appreciation. Performable works prescribe certain things to performers, and are appreciated for the qualities realizable in performances that satisfy these prescriptions. Theorists differ . . . as to the kinds of things that are prescribed and the nature of the things that do the prescribing.
>
> (Davies 2011: 87)

The "classical paradigm" can also be linked to Carl Dahlhaus's consideration of the modern work-concept as embracing four characteristic traits: (1) originality, (2) canonic status, (3) organic wholeness, and (4) aesthetic autonomy (Dahlhaus *et al.* 1984: 30–31).

2 The . . . *Bach* . . . project is an ongoing and expanding set of commissions that I started in 2014 as part of a larger interdisciplinary project, which included the ideas articulated in this book and a further series of audiovisual commissions that remain unfinished. For further reading, see http://robertoalonsotrillo.com/portfolio-item/bachproject/.

3 Nicolaus Listeninus's use of the phrase *opus perfectum et absolutum* can be found in his 1537 treatise *Musica*. The fragment reads:

> [P]oetic music . . . leaves some *opus* behind after the labour, as when music or a musical song is written by someone, whose goal is a complete and accomplished *opus*. For it consists in making or constructing, that is, in such labour that even after itself, when the artificer is dead, leaves a perfect and absolute opus.
>
> (Goehr 2007: 116)

In the final years of his life, Goethe prepared a complete revised edition of his works that he envisioned as definitive and complete, showing his last word on all his output. This collection, deeply influenced by the Romantic vision of the author–work relationship, was published under the *Ausgabe Letzter Hand*, the "Final Hand Edition" (Goethe 1827–1836). In this regard, see also Dadelson (1961).

4 John Kenneth Lutterman criticizes the Marxist undertones of the term "imperialism" and argues that the hegemony attributed to the work-concept would have been better understood if analyzed under the Gramscian concept of hegemony or Pierre Bourdieu's notion of *habitus* (Lutterman 2006: 47).

5 The notion of authorship marker can be connected to some of the ideas discussed in Chapter 2, amid the analysis of literary authorship theories during the second half of the twentieth century, such as the Foucaldian notion of author-function, Wayne Booth's discussion of the implied author, or Umberto Eco's conception of an open work. Nonetheless, the notion of authorship marker introduced here remains closer to Derrida's own intellectual world. In an interview in the French radio program *Le bon plaisir*, the French philosopher argued that:

> there is naturally a desire, for whoever speaks or writes, to sign in an idiomatic, that is, irreplaceable manner. But as soon as there is a mark, that is, the

> possibility of a repetition, as soon as there is language, generality has entered the scene and the idiom comprises with something that is not idiomatic: with a common language, concepts, laws, general norms . . . every discourse . . . carries with it a system of rules of producing analogous things and thus an outline of a methodology.
>
> (Derrida 1986)

6 In a broad sense, originality in the eighteenth century "was seen as a special form of imitation" (Lutterman 2006: 21). However, Bach's own conception of music and originality will be discussed in greater detail in Chapter 2. A tangentially connected yet telling example of the centrality and bearing of imitation at Bach's time can be found in Edward Young's 1759 essay "Conjectures on Original Composition" (Adams 1992: 338–347).

7 Adorno writes:

> The presumption that the musical means themselves have a historical tendency contradicts the traditional interpretation of the material of music. It is defined physicalistically in any event, in terms of a psychology of sound – as the sum total of sounds at the disposal of the composer. From this, however, the compositional material is as different as is speech from the inventory of its sounds. Not only does it contract and expand in the course of history. All of its specific traits are marks of the historical process. The more they bear historical necessity in themselves, the less they are immediately legible as historical traits.
>
> (Adorno 2006: 31)

For a further analysis of the development of the Adornian notion, see Paddison (1993: 65–96).

8 For further reading, see James Hepokoski's chapter on "Sonata Theory and Dialogic Form" in Caplin *et al.* (2010: 71–89).

References

Adams, Hazard, ed. *Critical Theory since Plato*. Boston: Cengage Learning, 1992.

Adorno, Theodor W. *Philosophy of New Music*. Minneapolis: University of Minnesota Press, 2006.

Barthes, Roland. *Image-Music-Text*. New York: Hill & Wang, 1977.

Caplin, William E., James Hepokoski, and James Webster. *Musical Form, Forms & Formenlehre: Three Methodological Reflections*. Leuven: Leuven University Press, 2010.

Cobussen, Marcel. "Deconstruction in Music." PhD diss., Erasmus University Rotterdam, 2002.

Dadelson, Georg von. "Die Fassung letzter Hand in der Musik." *Acta Musicologica* 33 (1961): 1–19.

Dahlhaus, Carl, Ruth E. Muller, and Friederick Zaminer. *Die Musiktheorie im 18. Und 19. Jahrhundert; Geschichte der Musiktheorie, Bd. 11*. Darmstadt: Wissenschaftliche Buchegesellschaft, 1984.

Davies, David. *Philosophy of the Performing Arts*. Oxford: Wiley-Blackwell, 2011.

Derrida, Jacques. "There Is No *One* Narcissism." Paris, 1986, available from http://hydra.humanities.uci.edu/derrida/narc.html

Erice, Víctor, and Abbas Kiarostami. *Erice-Kiarostami: Correspondences*. Barcelona: Centre de Cultura Contemporània de Barcelona, Institut d'Edicions de la Diputació de Barcelona and Actar, 2006.

Goehr, Lydia. *The Imaginary Museum of Musical Works: An Essay in the Philosophy of Music*. New York: Oxford University Press, 2007.

Goethe, Johann W. *Werke*. Stuttgart and Tübingen: Ausgabe Letzter Hand, 1827–1836.

Hepokoski, James, and Warren Darcy. *Elements of Sonata Theory: Norms, Types and Deformations in the Late Eighteenth Century Sonata*. New York: Oxford University Press, 2006.

Lutterman, John Kenneth. "Works in Progress: J. S. Bach's Suites for Solo Cello as Artifacts of Improvisatory Practices." PhD diss., University of California, 2006.

Paddison, Max. *Adorno's Aesthetics of Music*. New York: Cambridge University Press, 1993.

1 Poiesis

Overture

This chapter explores the nature of the filmic stimulus that led to conception of the . . . *Bach* . . . project and addresses the rationale behind my selection of Bach's Partita No. 1 for solo violin BWV 1002 as a case study. I briefly examine the elements that triggered my impetus to dispute the dominant notions of musical work and musical authorship and explain how such examination has been articulated in this specific case. Finally, I introduce a brief remark on the nature of the commissions of the . . . *Bach* . . . project before I posit the three central questions that the present book attempts to answer, a questioning critically linked to the overall reconsideration of the author- and work-concepts advanced here.

Filmic correspondences as impetus: questioning authorship

In 2005, two of the most intriguing film directors of the international panorama, Victor Erice and Abbas Kiarostami, started a filmic correspondence intended to inaugurate a new cinematographic format (Elena 2005; Arocena 1996). The outcome was so powerful that Barcelona's Centre of Contemporary Culture, among other Latin American cultural institutions, decided to expand it, increasing its generational and geographical scope: five further pairs of international directors were invited to collaborate.[1] These filmic correspondences formulated a return to an artisanal level of artistic creation, one that openly showcased those scars of the artistic tissue that remain usually hidden in the finished and commodified art- or filmwork: everything was work-in-progress, it was exposed cinema.

The *Correspondencia(s)* can also be understood as films about films, that is, a form of dialogic, self-reflective cinema. Every fragment echoes the previous one in a backward-looking gesture while introducing new material in a forward-looking gaze and inescapably reflecting on elements taken from the general thesaurus of cinematic history. Each film director explores potential connections without sacrificing her/his unique personal style; the emerging relationships are sometimes asymmetrical, swaying between the significance of iteration on the one hand and difference on the other. The spectator plays a crucial role in the conception of the correspondences. The exchanges might be intimate but not private; performance as a public arena of subjection becomes a key dimension of the newly emerging notion of authorship: only the reading to which they are exposed to under public display renders the *Correspondencia(s)* ultimately meaningful. The directors eventually understand that "they are creating a jointly vectorial work, one that seems to demand a closing gesture that helps the spectator infer that the correspondence has come to an end," even if such a gesture is forever denied (Ballo 2011). Individual authorship or at least its "normative" modern understanding is consequently powerfully contested.

The . . . *Bach* . . . project: questioning authorship?

Several elements, including the exemplar provided by the filmic correspondences and the study of the works and ideas of Roland Barthes and Jacques Derrida that I was undertaking at the time, supplied the initial impetus for the conception of the . . . *Bach* . . . project in 2014. Above all, I consider(ed) it necessary to question the anachronistic work- and author-concepts that I believe still permeate contemporary musicology, both at the conscious and – even more importantly – unconscious foundational levels.

Johann Sebastian Bach's Partita No. 1 provided an ideal case study as an instance of music about music, both in its internal structure – the *doubles* being elaborations of the main dance movements – and through the potential "external" contemporary continuation of its compositional model. The . . . *Bach* . . . project dialogically expands Bach's "artifact of improvisatory practices," adding three newly composed *doubles* to each of the four main dance movements, to integrate a total of twelve new expansions by twelve different international composers (see Table 1.1). In doing so, the project furthers Bach's original compositional gesture and raises several key musicological questions that ground the arguments explored in the remainder of this book. But before I move on to examine the contemporary development of authorship theories in the fields of literary criticism and musicology and present the intellectual framework based on Barthesian and Derridean ideas that will be employed in the concluding analytical section, I would like to introduce a brief consideration of the historical evolution of the partita/suite genre up to Bach's time. This analysis illustrates aspects of Bach's original

Table 1.1 The . . . *Bach* . . . project: complete list of composers

J. S. Bach	*i. Allemanda*	J. S. Bach	*ii. Corrente*
	Double		*Double*
Octavio Vázquez	*Double I*	Jesús Rueda	*Corrente Double*
Fernando Buide	*Doble*	Miguel Matamoro	*(...)*
Marco Stroppa	*Double III*	Henrik Denerin	*Zwischen der kürzeste Schatten*
J. S. Bach	*iii. Sarabande*	J. S. Bach	*iv. Tempo di Borea*
	Double		*Double*
Tomás Marco	*Double de double*	Seán Clancy	*Seven Minutes of Music on the Subject of Simulacra*
Carolina Noguera	*El doble del Doble*	Gabriel Erkoreka	*Boreal*
Juan P. Carreño	*Double III*	Esaias Järnegard	*Ymagino*

that will acquire a renewed transcendence as the text advances and its overall discursive structure unfolds and is consequently revealed.

The baroque suite and Bach's BWV 1002

According to the American musicologist David Fuller (b. 1927), the first recorded example of a group of pieces designated "suite" can be found in Estienne du Tertre's *Septième livre de danceries*, published in 1557 (Fuller 2016).[2] With a few exceptions, the printed music "constituted the raw material for practical use" as dance accompaniment, a material that interwove both dance and variation elements, which were either written or improvised (Ibid.). Throughout the late sixteenth and early seventeenth centuries, the stylistic developments in the different national schools and their reciprocation, which was especially significant in German-speaking lands, led to the emergence of what Fuller calls the "classical suite," which in its early stages comprised a three-part sequence of allemande, courante, and sarabande. The later addition of the gigue completed the standard four-dance combination, first realized in 1649 by Johann Jacob Froberger's Keyboard Suite No. 2.[3] Fuller points out that the "classical suite" status was not affected by "reduplication of the dances . . . the addition of doubles (variations), the interpolation of pieces among the basic four dances, and the presence of introductory movements" (Ibid.)[4]

J. S. Bach composed more than forty instrumental suites. Most were compiled in collections that systematically explored all of the genre's stylistic possibilities, each set becoming a "kind of thesaurus of the suite for that particular medium" (Ibid.).[5] Bach's suites combined two characteristic elements: the composer's masking of the genre's identity with textually intricate and technically challenging writing and a tendency to make "exercises" out of pieces in order to explore notational, stylistic, or contrapuntal resources. During the early stages of his compositional career, toward the end of the seventeenth century, Bach witnessed the development of a "mixed musical style" that blended elements of the French, Italian, and local traditions (Ledbetter 2009: 62–64). This mixed taste, or *vermischte Geschmack*, which eventually permeated the German scene, was exemplified by the influential output of Georg Philip Telemann or Georg Muffat. By the early eighteenth century, partially as a result of this idiomatic exchange, the suite would typically merge elements from the once markedly distinct sonata and dance genres. A tendency that is already evident in the late keyboard works of François Couperin, as it is in the music of the late German baroque composers.

Bach's Three Sonatas and Partitas for solo violin BWV 1001–1006, originally entitled *Sei Solo a Violino senza basso accompagnato*, were composed between 1703 and 1720, started during his Weimar days (1708–1717) and finally assembled during the composer's Cöthen period (1717–1723). Bach's *Sei Solo* might have been conceived as the first book – they are entitled *libro primo* – of a magnum opus that would have had included the Cello Suites as a *libro secondo*.[6] The set and its stylistic traits were certainly inspired by the great foregoing German tradition of music for solo violin with basso continuo or unaccompanied violin, exemplified in the works of Johann Heinrich Schmelzer (1623–1680), Heinrich Ignaz Franz Biber (1644–1704), Johann Jakob Walther (1650–1704), Johann Paul von Westhoff (1656–1705), Johann Joseph Vilsmayr (1663–1722), Johann Georg Pisendel (1687–1755), or in Georg Philipp Telemann's (1681–1767) *12 Fantasies*.[7] Paralleling the historical development of the *vermischte Geschmack*, the momentous repertoire of the German school emerged through a cross-fertilization of elements taken from the Italian violin tradition, the English viol school, and the remarkable native unwritten violin practices.

Bach's collection, which can be also seen as a violinistic idiomatic adaption of the composer's own keyboard polyphonic style, is divided into two groups of works: one that includes the three sonatas *da Chiesa* that follow the standard slow-fast-slow-fast movement sequence and a second one that comprises the three Partitas, which explore different movement combinations. According to the British Bach scholar Ruth Tatlow, the Sonatas and Partitas are "a textbook case of proportional parallelism," with the keys of the different solos forming "an allusion to Bach's name in the pattern B-A-C" (Tatlow 2015: 133). Tatlow asserts that the extremely clean manuscript must have been a copy of a now lost original and that, even if the score was not published at the time "such a polished, paginated autograph manuscript with title page and signature was the composer's equivalent of a publication and could . . . be lent for a fee to interested parties, or a sponsor could pay the composer to make a copy" (Ibid.: 134).[8] Tatlow has examined the perfect numerical proportions that underpin Bach's collection, exploring how the composer made changes to the final version of the score to achieve a thought-out balance with various carefully conceived overlapping layers of 1:1 and 1:2 ratios.

Bach's first Partita, BWV 1002, is an Italianate *Partia* that, while conceived as a *sonate da camera* that uses Italian movement-titles, intermingles elements of the French tradition. The Partita is an example of a solo instrumental suite type that pairs all its dances with their own *double*, following the French style, and replaces the closing Gigue with an unusual Tempo di Borea, imitating Corelli's preferred formula.[9] The *Partia* thus exemplifies, through the inclusion of the *doubles*, a form of inner variation based on a compositional principle that can be subjected to further development. That expansive gestures – which is also a rereading of Bach's original, a commentary, a displacement of his music into a newly forged public sphere, a de- and recontextualization, and a resultant reconsideration of its endless connotations and potential interpretations – is what the . . . *Bach* . . . project attempts to undertake.

Commissioning the . . . Bach *. . . project*

The original commissions of the . . . *Bach* . . . project were made in 2014 to the twelve international composers mentioned earlier. They were all approached with an introductory text that revealed only a few aspects of the larger picture that I was seeking to portray. An initial stress on the dialogic and epistolary dimensions of the project reflected my thoughts at the time. Those aspects, which followed the example of the *Correspondencia(s)* and of Derrida's book *The Post Card*, initially overshadowed my interest in questioning musical authorship and the work-concept:[10]

> I have already mentioned, at least to some of you, that I was planning to use the filmic correspondences initiated by Victor Erice and Abbas Kiarostami (through a proposal of Barcelona's Centre for Contemporary Culture), subsequently expanded by five further pairs of film directors and recently published by Intermedio (www.intermedio.net), as a structural reference. The epistolary dimension of the project is understood as a dialogue, an exposition of the creative process, of a rather craft-like phase that precedes that of the finished work. Such a dialogue

> can be established for, and based upon, a number of different reasons, from the rather practical one of working on a *doublé* with a common "main" movement to the potential existence of shared personal interests and may be articulated at an infinite number of levels, from tangential reflections on aspects that need not be specifically related to the project in hand to dialogues on specific aspects of the creative process.
>
> There are no apriorisms, no models to be followed, no methodological impositions, only an open dialogue that unfolds through time, a dialogue that I would like to present as a part of the project by way of a CD-Book. Such a catalogue is conceived to make the traditional line notes redundant, substituting them with a history of the reflection that accompanied, directly or indirectly, the temporal development of the project. We delve into an exchange – each letter watching or listening to the previous one – or we reject it – and we write letters with no addressee, personal notes – but, above all, we initiate an exchange that might be intimate but not private anymore. We want to create something that goes beyond the CD, to create a bond with the listener, to share a journey.

As I stressed earlier, this introductory text did not reveal the full nature of what the . . . *Bach* . . . project was intended to become. In the letter, I made no reference to this book or to the Barthesian and Derridean influences on my thinking and proposal, and I gave the composers absolute freedom in their choice of approach to their new *doubles*, to their expansion of Bach's music. Furthermore, the wording was intended to avoid any potential impact on their compositional decisions. But why did I conceal some aspects of the larger plan? I wanted to guarantee the composers' honest engagement both in their creative/compositional activities and in the letter exchange that they were about to establish with me. I did not want them to construct a mystified narrative designed to fit my plan but to expose their own narratives; my biases had to remain concealed if theirs were to be exposed. This was a necessary precondition to articulate my reflection on the nature of the work- and author-concepts. I was facing the problem of alterity and of the essential unknowability of the other, attempting to bridge, in the awareness of its impossibility, the distance between the composer's activities and ideas and their socioliterary construction as written-down text. I was attempting to create a shared space that explored a form of unconditional hospitality in its realization of the ineludible asymmetrical presence of its conditioned form. I was trying to bypass the inescapable spuriousness involved in the construction of the self as a self-reflective author that was involved in the act of "one writing about oneself." I did not want to mediate, or at least to be involved as little as possible, in the act of self-exposure implied by their yielding to the prospect of being read. Only once the manuscript had been finished were the composers allowed to write a reply to a text for them still unknown, a reply that became part of the dialogical textual design of Chapter 4.

Ritornello I

Now, as I hold a final (?) version of the score and the project has morphed and evolved to its current state, the time has come to raise and fathom three significant questions. First, can the . . . *Bach* . . . project be seen as a single work? Is it instead a sort of compositional collage – a puzzle? Or should it be considered somehow differently? Second, who would its author be? Is there one? Are there many? Is there any? And, finally, how can these preceding questions help us interrogate the dominant work- and author-concepts that permeate current musicological thought?

Notes

1 These were Jose Luis Guerin/Jonas Mekas, Albert Serra/Lisandro Alonso, Isaki Lacuesta/Naomi Kawase, Jaime Rosales/Wang Bing, and Fernando Eimbcke/So Yong Kim.

2 Estienne's score can be accessed from https://imslp.org/wiki/Danceries%2C_Livre_7_(Tertre%2C_Estienne_du). Let me remark here that I am solely referring to the classical suite, acknowledging that collections of dances or dance types can be found among some of the earliest examples of notated instrumental music.

3 This score can be accessed from: http://petrucci.mus.auth.gr/imglnks/usimg/9/9b/IMSLP33045-PMLP75280-6242710-Orgel-und-Klavierwerke-2-Johann-Jakob-Froberger.pdf. For further discussion of Froberger's work, see Starke (1972).

4 Even if this grants the suite structure a certain level of flexibility, Lutterman criticizes what he terms as Fuller's evolutionary formalist view and his notion of the "classical suite," an approach that distorts the flexibility that permeates the historical evolution of the suite to present it as an organically unified formal structure (Lutterman 2006: 185–186). Lutterman points out that "while suites organized along the lines of Froberger's gradually became more common, most collections of dances were published in a variety of formats that do not lend themselves to easy categorization" (Lutterman 2006: 193).

5 These sets would include solo keyboard works such as the English Suites BWV 806–811, the French Suites BWV 812–817, and the Six Partitas BWV 825–830 as well as Bach's Six Suites for solo cello BWV 1007–1012.

6 This is discussed in Jones (2013: 93). A different argument is introduced by Ruth Tatlow, who points out that "as the Six Sonatas are such an exact numerical and structural parallel to the Six Solos . . . Bach intended the Six Sonatas for violin and harpsichord to the primary matching collection, with the Cello Suites as a possible *Libro Terzo*" (Tatlow 2015: 141).

7 Specific examples include Schmelzer's *Sonatae unarum fidium* (1664) and his *Ciaccona* (1670) for unaccompanied violin, Biber's *Mistery Sonatas* (c. 1676)

with its crowning *Passacalgia* for solo violin, Walther's *Hortulus chelicus* (1688), Westhoff's *Six Suites for Unaccompanied Violin* (1696), Vilsmayr's *Six Partitas* (published in 1715), several pieces from Pisendel's Dresden collection, and Telemann's *12 Fantasies,* which were published in 1735, after Bach's *Sonatas and Partitas*, but are representative of Telemann's highly influential style.

8 As a matter of fact, we have a copy made in 1726 of an early version of the *Sei Solo* by Johann Peter Kellner and a transcription of the original manuscript made by Anna Magdalena Bach for Georg Heinrich Ludwig Schwanberg between 1727 and 1731.

9 For a study of the numerical proportions underpinning this Partita and its relationship to those found in the first Sonata, see Tatlow (2015: 136–140).

10 Derrida defined *The Post Card* as a "satire of epistolary literature" (Derrida 1987).

References

Arocena, Carmen. *Víctor Erice*. Madrid: Ediciones Catedra, 1996.

Ballo, Jordi, ed. *Correspondencias*. Barcelona: Prodimag S. L., 2011.

Derrida, Jacques. *The Postcard: From Socrates to Freud and Beyond.* Chicago: University of Chicago Press, 1987.

Elena, Alberto. *The Cinema of Abbas Kiarostami*. London: Saqui Books, 2005.

Fuller, David. "Suite." *Grove Music Online: Oxford Music Online*. Oxford University Press, 2016, accessed January 19, 2018, www.oxfordmusiconline.com/subscriber/article/grove/music/27091

Jones, Richard D. P. *The Creative Development of Johann Sebastian Bach.* New York: Oxford University Press, 2013.

Ledbetter, David. *Unaccompanied Bach: Performing the Solo Works*. New Haven, CT: Yale University Press, 2009.

Lutterman, John Kenneth. "Works in Progress: J. S. Bach's Suites for Solo Cello as Artifacts of Improvisatory Practices." PhD diss., University of California, 2006.

Starke, Davie. *Frobergers Suitentänze*. Darmstadt, Germany: Tonos Editions, 1972.

Tatlow, Ruth. *Bach's Numbers: Compositional Proportion and Significance*. Cambridge: Cambridge University Press, 2015.

2 Authorship and workhood

Intellectual framework

Transition

This chapter opens with an exploration of the key developments in authorship theories in the literary field during the second half of the twentieth century, an exploration that grounds the intellectual framework developed in Chapter 3. I move on to examine Lydia Goehr's critical analysis of the historical emergence of the work- and author-concepts, regulative concepts that, I argue, still permeate contemporary musicology. I proceed to summarize recent questionings of those Romantic notions that, while partially paralleling the example provided by literary criticism, have been predominantly undertaken from ontological perspectives. These analyses point towards potential *loci* of intellectual confluence and lead to a final consideration of the analytical perspectives introduced in the following chapters, a consideration that enables me to raise preliminary answers to the key question(s) posited by this text: how can the . . . *Bach* . . . project be used to reassess the notions of musical work and musical authorship?

Authorship and literary authorship theories in the late twentieth century

Some of the most substantial developments in authorship theories that have taken place during the past sixty years originated within the fields of literary theory and literary criticism before they permeated other artistic disciplines. This section introduces a brief historical summary of those theoretical shifts, a summary designed to ground the ensuing consideration of the dominant notion of musical workhood and authorship by exposing possible paths of revision and critique. I take a combination of Dario Compagno and Andrew Bennett's division of those historical developments into three different phases as a referential analytical framework (see Table 2.1 in the Annex), which is nuanced and expanded with other significant discussions of literary authorial theory found in recent scholarship (Bennett 2005; Compagno 2012).[1] The present focus on literary theories seeks to link this fragment to the subsequent analysis of Barthesian and Derridean ideas, introduced in Chapter 3.

Phase 1: phenomenology, formalism, and New Criticism

The first of these phases emerges from a phenomenologist approach based on the ideas of the German philosopher Edmund Husserl (1859–1938) and his crucial differentiation between intention and meaning – that is, between the experiences of those who speak and write and the public meaning of their words (Husserl 1970: 187–189). In this first phase:

> intentions are private and contingent: they are important for everyday life . . . but also impossible to communicate to others. Language allows a private mental state . . . to set up a link with another private mental state . . . because meanings are independent from private intentions: meanings live in sentences and texts, and resist time.
>
> (Compagno 2012: 40)

Springing from that phenomenological tradition, the overlapping schools of Russian Formalism and New Criticism, which can be seen as part of a broader school of formalist literary criticism, coincided in their search for a certain purity that rejected the question of authorship as pertaining to interpretation (Bennett 2005: 74). This approach determined the conception of authorship distinctive of some of the major figures of American New Criticism, such as William Wimsatt (b. 1941) and Monroe Beardsley (1915–1985). Their anti-intentionalist theory, linked to the notion of the "intentional fallacy,"[2] did not imply, however, a categorical negation of authorial intentionality, even if meaning was conceived as independent from the author's design. Instead, New Criticists argued that meaning had to be encapsulated in the text, becoming effective within it, and that, as a result, it could only be reached from an intrinsic/intratextual and not an extrinsic/extratextual reading.

Phase 2: from the death of the author to the reemergence of intentionality

The second phase results from the radical revision of Wimsatt's and Beardsley's ideas undertaken by French intellectuals such as Roland Barthes (1915–1980) and Jacques Derrida (1930–2004). This reconsideration involves the abandonment of the possibility of an objective analysis in favor of what Dario Compagno terms "anarchical multi-disciplinary readings of the text" (Compagno 2012: 41).[3] Barthes brings the previously dominant understanding of the author to an end by negating the need of a master meaning (Barthes 1977: 142–148). The notion of authorship that permeated New Criticism is thus radically transformed; the "author's intentions . . . [stop being] the idiosyncratic variation against which one should look for an ideal and objective meaning; now, the author is the ideal and objective meaning, dull limit that has no value for criticism" (Compagno 2012: 41).[4] Meaning loses its idealized objective and durable dimension and becomes fluid, the analytical focus moving from the conscious to the unconscious level of the writer's (or, in this case, composer's) psyche and its relationship to the text. The rejection of objective meanings contests the centrality of the phenomenological meaning/intention dualism. In her/his new role, the critic "follows traces and hints, reaching meanings and thoughts that could have been in the author"; interpretation consequently becomes informed guessing.

Derrida, following and critically expanding Barthes's project, negated the possibility of an isolated "ideal dimension of meaning that excludes all contingent references, leaving only pure thought" (Compagno 2012: 42).[5] His vision rejected as well stable meanings and challenged the understanding of the text as a single, monolithic message, through an investigation of the writer's unconscious, advocating a renewed centrality of the reader's role as an active element in the construction of the textual, of textuality. Derrida proposed all texts inexorably are examples of undecidability and that they consequently betray any meaning that an author might attempt to impose upon them: "the writer writes *in* a language and *in* a logic whose proper system, laws, and life his discourse by definition cannot dominate absolutely. He uses them only by letting himself . . . be governed by the system" (Derrida 1976: 158).[6] Derrida's search for a fallible author ignited the theoretical move from an idealized hypertrophic author to a humanized one (Compagno 2012: 43).

A new critical reading of Barthes's and Derrida's notions lead to a nuanced reintroduction of the significance of the author's intention as it is shaped through her/his texts. The key analytical focus of this new theoretical approach became the examination of that process of emergence. Michel Foucault (1926–1984), the first significant figure to confront the notion of authorship that permeated the previous readings, argued that since subjectivity cannot predate language, it must necessarily emerge from "cultural production and interpretation" (Ibid.: 44). The author is not to be found within the isolated text but can only be tracked in one that has been historically and culturally contextualized. The notion of the author-function thus arises as "the interface between a text and the system of other relevant texts in which is it is produced" (Ibid.). Texts need to be read as part of larger cultural regularities. Foucault argues that it is a matter of depriving the author-subject of "its role as originator, and of analyzing the subject as a complex and variable function of discourse" (Foucault 1984: 118).[7] Both the concept of cultural regularities and the centrality of the interpreter play a crucial role in modeling Foucault's notion of authorship.

Compagno points out, in an analysis of Foucault's authorship theory, that the "author-function" can be seen as the sum of all constraints to writing, the "negative half" of the human author. The next significant contribution to authorship theory, the work of the American literary critic Wayne Booth (1921–2005), would invert this by focusing on the "positive half" (Compagno 2012: 45). Booth, departing from the idea of "intentional fallacy" inherited from the previously discussed premises of American New Criticism, reinstalled a notion of intentionality linked to an exploration of the author's choices, which become meaningful analyzable traces. Booth defines what he terms the "implied author" as "the sum of his own choices" (Booth 1961: 74). Meaning is not idealized, as in Husserl's reading, or a by-product of the unconscious workings of the author's psyche; it is the result of a conscious yet culturally constrained creative activity that necessarily leaves traces of the author's intentionality.

Feminist literary criticism would also become increasingly significant throughout the 1970s. Elaine Showalter (b. 1941), a key representative of the movement, coined the term "gynocriticism" in her essay "Feminist Criticism in the Wilderness" (1981) to refer to the study of women *as writers* (Showalter 1986: 243–270). While some feminist readings would be at odds with Barthesian authorship and the idea of the death of the author, others would welcome it as an act of liberation from an oppressive patriarchal construct. The first group argued that, since the negation of authorial identity rendered the gender perspective unnecessary, it did not apply to the already denied authority of female writers. As a result, the deconstruction of the author could "be seen, in effect, as the deconstruction of the masculine author, part of the deconstruction of a certain thinking of masculinity, of patriarchy itself" (Bennett 2005: 85).[8] Feminist post-structuralists, on the other hand, would criticize such a perspective as an adaptation and continuation of a patriarchal discourse, claiming that to undo the "patriarchal practice of *authority*," they had to "proclaim with Roland Barthes the death of the author" (Moi 1985: 62–63). Moreover, the *écriture feminine* theorized and practiced by the French writers Luce Irigary (b. 1930), Heléne Cixous (b. 1937), and Julia Kristeva (b. 1941) in the mid-1970s asserted "not the sexuality of the text but the textuality of sex" (Jacobus 1986: 109). In doing so, their perspective avoided essentialism and biological determinism, developing a sense of femininity as "constructed or assumed . . .

[T]he author herself is part of a performance of subjectivity, of subjectivity as gendered" (Bennett 2005: 87).

Phase 3: public intentionality, the text as interpretation, and New Historicism

Both Foucault's and Booth's theories and the rise of "gynocriticism" mark the transition to the third phase, one that attempts to find a balance between the author's phenomenological consciousness and her/his (post)structural unconscious. Their use of neologisms ("author-function" and "implied author") or surrogates, as Compagno refers to them, might show that, despite their critical effort, the idea of a "real author," one that cannot be reached through analysis, remains present, even if "the image of the author emerging from a text is necessarily different from what the author really is" (Compagno 2012: 46). In this third phase, a semiotization of intention leads to the emergence of its public life, the "real author" disappears; now "all of the man is in the work" (Ibid.). This approach was first developed by Jacques Bouveresse (b. 1940), who found in Ludwig Wittgenstein's arguments the first contestation of what he termed the "myth of interiority."[9] It was nonetheless Elisabeth Anscombe (1919–2001), one of Wittgenstein's students, who was the first to develop "an explicit theory of action onto what is publicly done and interpreted" (Ibid.: 47).[10] If intentions are understood as exclusively public, a new teleological notion of the author necessarily arises, one in which the author becomes "a series of answers given to the question why, asked about a text from many possible perspectives. Without this question, a text would not be such" (Ibid.: 48).

Luigi Pareyson (1918–1991), who envisioned artistic intention as the outcome of interpretative readings, expanded Anscombe's theories: intentions emerge during the creative process and persist in the work but need to be reactivated by the interpreter if the work is to be understood.[11] The Italian semiotician and literary critic Umberto Eco (1932–2016) followed a similar argument to introduce a vision of intentionality as a precondition of art, claiming that "the original gesture, fixed by and in the sign, is in itself a direction that will eventually lead us to the discovery of the author's intention" (Eco 1989: 102). Eco stressed that "public" intention, which is semiotic in nature, grants the interpreter a limited amount of freedom; yet if a work escapes the author's command, it begins to generate its own meaning, and what remains "is no longer a field of possibilities but rather the indistinct, the primary, the indeterminate at its wildest – at once everything and nothing" (Ibid.: 93). Openness thus becomes an essential trait of language and thinking – one that negates a completely conscious and author-controlled/closed intentionality but that nonetheless grants it some "directive power."

As a result, interpretation becomes a "matter of recognizing [both] what is intentional: where the work begins and ends, and what is planned within it," as well as what is unintentional (Compagno 2012: 50). The interpreter's analytical balancing of intentionality and nonintentionality makes possible different readings of the same text.

Foucault's authorial theory and the influence of other post-structuralist notions can be linked to the emergence of New Historicism, a turn to a textualized historicism exemplified by the work of Louis Montrose (b. 1950) and Stephen Greenblatt (b. 1943). In New Historicism, "the author's consciousness, his or her subjectivity or intention, even his or her life, are conceived as historical and textual, subject to and subject of the discursive dynamics of the circulations of power" (Bennett 2005: 90). Their negation of the Romantic autonomous individual author and the Romantic work-concept is paired with an interest in the subjectivities of social beings, in a newly socialized author. The author thus becomes a regulating presence understood from a textually and socio-historically embedded perspective, an author conceived from her/his otherness. As Greenblatt points out, within the perspective granted by the consideration of the author as a social being:

> actions that appear to be single are disclosed as multiple; the apparently isolated power of the individual genius turns out to be bound up with collective, social energy; a gesture of dissent may be an element in a larger legitimation process, while an attempt to stabilize the order of things may turn out to subvert it.
>
> (Greenblatt 1990: 164–165)

Transition

This historical overview introduces a valuable referential framework that grounds the arguments developed in the subsequent sections of the book. Phenomenology and New Historicism have been chosen here as the two cardinal poles that demarcate the options explored by the ensuing musicological approaches. It is fundamental to understand and remember that every redefinition of authorship is necessarily linked to a new understanding of the work, the text, and the textual (and vice versa). Even if the literary focus on meaning and intention, especially with regard to the public dimension of intentionality, has provided powerful examples for the reconsideration of authorship in music, a thorough reassessment of music's textuality remains to be undertaken.[12] It is there that an examination of Barthesian and Derridean intellectualities, given the sharp formulation accorded in their writings to the question of the textual and textuality, might prove to be a significant contribution. But first I would like to examine the dominant notions of musical authorship and work-concept that permeate contemporary musicology, tracing their historical origin and contrasting them with those new readings that have emerged from or might have been influenced by the developments in literary theory considered thus far.

On music and authorship

The work-concept and Goehr's conceptual imperialism

A fundamental question, regarding the relationship between literary and musicological scholarship, emerges from the historical perspective sketched thus far: why has the impact of literary authorship theories on musicological discourses been so limited during the past few decades? Some scholars would argue that the semiotic differences between literature and music introduce an inescapable adaptive limitation.[13] I argue instead that the theoretical shifts that have marked the development of the conception of authorship in literature could have exerted a greater influence on musicological discourses without a necessary reconsideration of the nature of such semiotic dissimilarities.[14] As a matter of fact, the notion of authorship that permeates most twentieth-century musical scholarship, in which the modern work-concept plays a central role, is an ossified remnant from the Romantic period.[15] Such Romantic idealizations of the composer and the work, which will be explored in this section, emerged parallel to the notion of the Romantic literary author, an "author" contested by all the literary theories explored thus far.[16]

In *The Imaginary Museum of Musical Works*, Lydia Goehr examines the historical development of the understanding of the work-concept.[17] Goehr argues that its current bearing gained critical centrality within a specific historical context before it came to be applied as an inescapable categorizer to music of all periods through what she terms a form of "conceptual imperialism" (Goehr 2007: 345–253). Moreover, it "emerged in line with the development of numerous other concepts, some of which are subsidiary – performance-of-a-week, score, and composer – some of which are oppositional – improvisation and transcription. It also emerged alongside the rise of ideals of accurate notation and perfect compliance. In this process, the work-concept achieved the most central position" (Ibid.: 103). Goehr points out that both the work- and the associated composer/author-concepts have a regulative force: their apparently incontestable comprehensibility conceals an elusive meaning. Both their seemingly absolute nature and the fact that they underpin and regulate our musical practices make such concepts difficult to question, according to Goehr, since:

> These concepts function stably because they are treated as givens and not "merely" as concepts that have artificially emerged and crystallized within a practice . . . we simply think about them as absolute . . . to avoid the challenge of a threatening opposition or the challenge of relativists . . . from within the practice, regulative concepts are seen to be self-legitimating.
>
> (Ibid.: 104–105)

The work- and author-concepts have thus receded into the unmovable foundational assumptions of the musically unconscious even if they have a continuous and direct impact on the level of the musically conscious (on musicology, on performance, etc.). Furthermore, the modern dominant notion of the work-concept implies a theorization of a practice that does not take into account the real structure of the theorized practice, a dangerous fissure emerging between both – even if following Goehr, we admit that practice "ultimately remains theorized, as theory ultimately remains practiced" (Ibid.: 107).

Goehr stresses that, from a historical point of view, the usage of the term *opus perfectum* by Nikolaus Listenius in his treatise *Musica*, published in 1527, should not be seen as an early reference that might have foreshadowed the emergence of the Romantic work-concept.[18] As a matter of fact, from the Aristotelian perspective that was dominant at the time, Listenius's *opus* could be defined as "the product of performance, not just the pre-existing idea that brings a performance about" (Goehr 2007: 117). Goehr's central claim is that the work-concept emerged in the 1800s even if:

> [terms used prior to 1800] came to be synonymous or nearly so with the term "work". "Piece", "composition", "opus", are examples. But again, unless the evidence can support it, one cannot assume that all these terms and uses of concepts indicate that musicians were thinking predominantly about music in terms of works.
>
> (Ibid.: 119)

The understanding of music that permeated Antiquity and the Middle Ages continued to wield its power up to the late eighteenth century. It was only through the emancipation of music from the extramusical that the modern work-concept appeared through a synthesis of elements from two preexisting realms: music and the productive arts. Music stopped being conceived as an art of skilled performance to become an "art that resulted from the activity of composition not just in performances but also in works of art" (Ibid.: 151). Under Romantic aesthetics, music was forced to adopt the product-based nature of its sister disciplines as a requisite to rejoin the "league" of the fine arts. Two main elements impacted this novel understanding of music, "a transcendent move from the worldly and particular to the spiritual and universal . . . [and a] formalist move which brought meaning from music's outside to its inside" (Ibid.: 153). As a result, the new Romantic aesthetic "allowed music to mean its purely musical self at the same time that it meant everything else" (Ibid.: 157). Following the preceding argument, Goehr concludes:

> The purported autonomy of the fine arts, guaranteed by their placement in museums, raised particularly interesting problems for music. These become apparent as we begin to consider how music came to replicate the characteristics of the plastic arts of painting and sculpture. As it entered the world of the fine arts, music had to find a plastic or equivalent commodity, a valuable and permanently existing product that could be treated in the same way as the objects of the already respectable fine arts. Music would have to find an object that could be divorced from everyday contexts, form a part of a collection of works of art, and be contemplated purely aesthetically. Neither transitory performances nor incomplete scores would serve this purpose since, apart from anything else, they were worldly or at least transitory and concrete items. So an object was found through projection or hypostatization. The object was called the "work."
>
> (Goehr 2007: 173–174)

Critiques of Goehr's approach

Since Goehr's evaluation of the emergence of the modern work-concept as a culturally and historically contingent idea, which has been defined by Lutterman as an "exercise in polemic hyperbole," has provoked significant musicological controversy, I would like to explore and assess some of the most compelling challenges raised to her approach in order to clarify my own critical standpoint (Lutterman 2006: 11).

Scholars Leeman L. Perkins and Reinhard Strohm, among others, have pointed out the "frailty of several of [the book's] historiographical arguments" (Strohm in Talbot 2000: 138). Perkins asserts, referring to Goehr's exploration of Listenius's 1537 treatise *Musica* as historical evidence, that at that point in history, the work-concept was commonly used and discernible, and employed to refer to "a musical work as an identifiable ontological entity" (Perkins 2002: 16). His approach connects the emergence of the work-concept to the increasing historical reliance on musical notation, its increasing specificity, the increasing recognition given to the composer as author/creator and to the role played by the objectual commodification of music as score that resulted from the emergence and development of the musical press. According to Perkins, the medieval traditions that permeate Listenius's treatise are already marked by a distinction of music as extemporization/performative practice and music as a notated score, music as *mentaliter* and music as *scripto* to employ the terms used in Johannes Tinctoris's 1496 *Practica Musicae*: "it is evident . . . that Tinctoris attached special ontological significance to such compositions, seeing them as comparable in a very real sense to the literary work of classical antiquity to which he so frequently refers" (Ibid.: 23). Furthermore, this supposed understanding of individual compositions as "complete in and of themselves" was also reflected by the characteristic precision of the scribes when dealing with an original text and the significance given by music theorists to the reliability of the sources, Perkins mentioning Heinrich Glarean's *Dodecachordon* as an example (Ibid.: 26).[19]

A further critique is raised against Goehr's claim that links the emergence of the work-concept to the development of autonomous instrumental forms that were independent from any form of word setting, a claim that contradicts, he argues, the available historical evidence. Perkins dates the first examples of purely instrumental music in the sixteenth century (the earliest purely instrumental idiomatic examples being the *ricercari* of Francesco Spinacino and Joan Ambrosio Danza) stressing that:

> textless composition began to emerge from an earlier improvisatory practice that depended a good deal more on memory than on written notes. What had been largely a performer's art was transformed in relatively short order by the fixity needed for the notational process.
>
> (Ibid.: 30)

Among the instrumental genres that emerged after the 1500s, such as the *fantasias* or the Iberian *tientos*, Perkins includes the stylization of dance music, which, as we have seen, was used not only as musical accompaniment but as purely instrumental elaboration.

The normalization of the employment of the opus number as a way to structure a composer's oeuvre, as exemplified by early baroque Italian composers such as Biagio Marini or Giovanni Legrenzi and by Arcangello Corelli's influential case, denotes "that the attention and polish needed to prepare such compositions for publication bestowed on them a distinctive status, not unlike that we are inclined to attribute to musical works in the present day" (Ibid.: 34). Perkins stresses that his consideration of the historical evidence "would suggest that the status of 'work' meant at the time that every detail that could be fixed notationally was considered an essential part of the piece, to be written as accurately and interpreted as scrupulously as possible" (Ibid.: 41).

Reinhard Strohm raises a similar argument when he points out that Goehr's critique draws the 1800 watershed-line as an *a priori* analytical assumption and that, as a result, her historical perspective "involves the fending off of rival claims on the work-concept arising from earlier practices (and a little from modern and post-modern times, where the argument is, however, carried off convincingly)" (Strohm in Talbot 2000: 141). Strohm explains that Goehr's critical reading of Listenius emerges from a historical misinterpretation that does not take into account the classical background of the idea of *musica poetica* and claims that Renaissance humanists "introduced the concept of the musical work as a regulative concept by transferring its general idea from the classical tradition of the other arts," as exemplified by the music and musical practices of Franco-Netherlandish composers from Dufay to Josquin (Ibid.: 142).[20] What distinguishes the earlier employment of the work-concept from its Romantic form is a quantitative matter, according to Strohm, and the philosophically distinct statuses given to both attempts to trace a metahistorical argument that is "deduced from mere cultural history" (Ibid.: 145). From that perspective, Goehr's argument against conceptual imperialism becomes tautological since it could be laid at the author's own door.

One further critical standpoint has been introduced by John Kenneth Lutterman, who defines Goehr's historical ontology as an eclectic and post-modern approach. Lutterman supports Goehr's vision of the work-concept as open, regulative, projective, and emergent but, following Strohm and Perkins, criticizes her analysis of the historical shift of the relationship between musical practice ideals and the work-concept around and after the 1800s, an analysis that is at once homogenizing, not well historically grounded, and based on questionable evidence. Lutterman stresses that "Goehr's claim is more subtly nuanced and complex than some of her detractors have recognized . . . [but] her elucidation of the hegemony of such a monolithic 'regulative' concept seems a retreat to the very kind of transcendental analytic ontology that she set out to critique" (Lutterman 2006: 66).

As Goehr's critiques rightly point out, one of the most challenging aspects of the classical Western music tradition in the seventeenth and early eighteenth centuries, an aspect that is fundamental to a historicist consideration of the work- and author-concepts, is what John Butt defines as the "very fluidity of musical practice" (Butt and Carter 2005: 27). Such flexibility was linked to the variability of "local" performance practice traditions, a malleability that went beyond the potential of the notational means to fix performance parameters. A consideration of these seminal concepts is further complicated by the different approaches that have emerged toward the consideration of the relationship between musical canonization and workhood.[21] While various scholars have argued, as we have seen, that an underpinning transhistorical continuity of a variable work-concept that has evolved through different definitions and regulative roles permeates the European tradition,[22] this development might not correspond to the modern vision of progress as teleologically linear since, as John Butt points out, "abstract composerly thinking extends well beyond the rigorous counterpoint of the ricercar, while even so hardened a musical form as the concerto or the da-capo aria might often be the platform for what is essentially a performance-based genre" (Ibid.: 33). Following this argument, a historical shift, with regard to the distinction between composer- and performer-related genres and the underlying notions of work and event, might have taken place between a predominance of the first type in the late sixteenth century, of the second during the seventeenth, and a return to the sixteenth-century paradigm in the nineteenth. Thus, the reification of musical works was not the result of a constant and/or linear process, even if we accept that:

> the seventeenth century saw a greater concretization of individually, formally structured pieces, this was clearly something distinct from the comparative notational fixity formerly achieved through print, especially given that publications that did present a comparatively "finished" version of the score, such as Corelli's celebrated prints, often appeared well after the music had been formed in manuscript and by way of multiple performances.
>
> (Ibid.: 36)[23]

Some of these arguments might be used to support Goehr's antiteleological perspective and her critique of the so-called Wiggish approach to history, even if we admit that her perception of music before 1800 homogenizes musical practices, being insufficiently documented and thus historically grounded.[24] Butt points out that the understanding of authorship and individuality in the seventeenth century was fluid and contradictory, a contradiction that grounded a vision of compositional perfection "that tended to work against the idea of the composer as original genius" (Ibid.: 43). As a matter of fact, one of the key notions that permeated compositional individuality in the sixteenth and seventeenth centuries was that of *imitatio*, an imitation of exemplary models intended to expand the perfection of the arts. Even if music theory in the eighteenth century reflected the increasing significance of individuality and originality, we could nonetheless contrast their vision of music as a continuation of "natural" order and the Romantic stress on the separation between the world of art and reality.

The fact that a work-concept might have existed prior to Goehr's debatable 1800 "watershed" and that it might have had a distinctive ontological status does not imply that such a concept was necessarily identical with the one that emerged, or evolved from it, in the late eighteenth and early nineteenth centuries. My supporting contention is twofold: on the one hand, I argue that we find a shift on the underpinning conceptualization of the relationship between the composer and the score as a written text and, on the other, a shift on the relationship between composition as written-down practice and performance as pure replication of that mnemonic material. Even if we assume that within the "context of the European tradition, there is . . . an essential transhistorical unity implied by the work-concept," that does not imply that its regulative nature has been historically stable (Ibid.: 28).[25]

Bach as an author

The question remains: how does Bach's conception of music and, more specifically, of the BWV 1002 fit within Goehr's argument? The answer is not simple. Chronologically, we could argue that Bach's work predates the ascension to a ubiquitous predominance of the modern work-concept and the Romantic ideal of authorial individualism. On the other hand, various elements seem to counter a performance-based understanding of music: the Partita was conceived as part of a set, it was not written for a specific occasion, and there is no historical record proving that it was ever performed during the composer's lifetime.[26] However, we know that, as a renowned teacher, Bach published an important part of his solo music as *Übungen*, exercises that had a pedagogical aim both at the performative and compositional levels; even if his *Sei Solo a Violino* BWV 1001–1006 are not labeled as such, they play a similar role as a display or exercise of compositional mastery. We also know that the Partita model stems from a historical tradition characterized by a significant level of compositional flexibility, one linked to Lutterman's discussion of "artifacts of improvisatory practices" and based on a format of internal variation that remains arguably open to further elaboration.[27] In addition, the numerous examples provided by Bach's appropriation of the music of other composers and by the continuous recycling of his own showcase an understanding of authorship that differs in essence from the one that emerged in the late seventeenth century from what Goehr terms as "romantic aesthetics."[28] All of these elements point toward two further critical questions that need to be answered before we move on to explore the dominant work- and author-concepts that permeate contemporary musicology: how much do we know about Bach's understanding of composition? And how could that help us define his conception of authoriality and workhood?

Since Bach did not write much about his own perception of music, any analysis of his understanding of authorship and workhood must be inferred from his scores and from historically relevant secondary sources.[29] By studying his manuscripts, we come to realize that, as the German musicologist Werner Breig points out, "at every period of his creative life Bach can be found altering, arranging, and continuing to develop his own and other composer's works" (Breig in Butt 1997: 154). Bach's music is permeated by (sometimes parodic) revisions, adaptations, and arrangements that show a material- rather than concept-focused understanding and theorizing of composition and the compositional process.[30] From this point of view, a significant part of his output can be seen as a continuous revision guided by an essential surpassing or perfecting principle, a work-in-progress not necessarily linked to the composer's vision of his own music and scores as fixed and reified but as a fluid dialogic arena. Thus, inasmuch as Bach's ideas frequently point to the world outside the work, the Suites and Partitas should not be approached as "manifestations of an isolated, autonomous artistic imagination . . . [but as] evidence of Bach in dialogue with his world, engaging the musical ideas of other composers and cultures, and responding to the utterances of other voices" (Lutterman 2006: 100).

Bach's transcriptions of Vivaldi's music for organ and harpsichord exemplify the composer's dialogue with the music of his contemporaries. Referring to the German's work on those transcriptions, Johann Nikolaus Forkel, his first biographer, pointed out that:

> he studied the chain of ideas, their relation to each other, the variations of the modulations, and many other particulars. The change necessary to be made in the ideas and passages composed for the violin, but not suitable to the clavier, taught him to think musically; so that after his labour was completed, he no longer needed to expect his ideas from his fingers, but derive them from his own fancy.
>
> (Forkel 1950: 38–40)

By thinking musically, Forkel invoked Bach's ability to reduce particular musical ideas found in a specific composition to their purely musical dimension, to their essential traits, in order to be modified and reproduced in different contexts, a technique that grounded as well Bach's improvisatory practices. Bach's approach, as the remainder of the book endeavors to demonstrate, has much in common with that permeating the . . . *Bach* . . . project.

One further key element of Bach's compositional approach is the significant employment of different forms of iteration – such as ornamental variation, which maintains the essence of the original material, and inflected variation, which alters its meaning – as building tools. As the American Bach scholar Laurence Dreyfus points out, "for Bach and his German contemporaries, the act of thinking through the fundamental music blocks of a composition fell under the rhetorical rubric of inventio, which since ancient times had been concerned with the discovery of ideas" (Dreyfus in Butt 1997: 173). Dreyfus thus sees unpredictability as a key aspect of a significant part of Bach's output, an aspect that differentiates his music from that distinctive of the late eighteenth-century sonata paradigm, which was governed by clear tonal and motivic teleologies. Inventiveness is praised over dramatic construction, and the Bachian puzzle, in lieu of a bidimensional juxtaposition of fragments, becomes a "three-dimensional space in which all individual pieces (that is, musical passages or inventions) are joined both above and below as well as next to one another, as both paradigms and syntagms" (Ibid.: 175). Consequently, Bach's compositional activity cannot be theorized as creation *ex nihilo*: it becomes instead an ingenious selection of the mechanisms of invention, a humanly creative encounter with a compositional machinery.

A unique aspect of Bach's writing style for solo instrument, exemplified in his BWV 1002, was the extreme level of notational precision. As I pointed out earlier, such notational specificity might have had a pedagogical aim, a text intended to serve as a manual of improvisatory skills or *Manieren* for the advanced or *geübte* musicians, a text located on the now clearly demarcated frontier between composition and improvisation. From that perspective, Bach's Suites/Partitas should not be examined under the modern work-concept lens but as artifacts of improvisatory practices, artifacts that might have represented coetaneous professional practices more accurately than written treatises managed to. They are, following John Lutterman, "valuable traces of practices of solo performing, practices that were once quite widespread, but which by their very nature are difficult to document" (Lutterman 2006: 1).[31] At a time when an important part of the ornamentation was unspecified and extemporized, Bach's approach to notational specificity, which was not the standard practice, became a referent for the following generation of canonic composers. It thus seems clear, once again, that "many of our most widespread assumptions about the nature of musical texts and their relation to the practice of music in Bach's day differ in important ways from those of Bach and his contemporaries" (Ibid.: 19).

Transition

So, to what extent are the modern work- and author-concepts incompatible with Bach's music? Is that incompatibility extensible to music from any period? How does it affect the relationship between the different facets of music? My thesis is that what underpins the modern work-concept and the centrality of the textual dimension of the score is a notion of textuality – a type of text fetishism permeated by critical standards of closure, unity, and autonomy – that is not fully compatible with the nature of music and musicking.[32] In this musical museum culture, "texts, the artifacts of musical practices, are reified as works, as autonomous aesthetic objects [and] best understood in isolation from the intrusions of human agency" (Ibid.: 34).[33] Furthermore:

> with a prior understanding of the score as a fixed, quasi-sacred masterwork simply taken for granted, it has been easy to dismiss or devalue any evidence not recorded directly in notation . . . the task of interpretation has often been approached as if the treatises were simple decoder rings.
> (Ibid.: 96)

It is on the articulation of a new textuality of music, linked to the ongoing questioning of authorship, that the ideas of Barthes and Derrida will prove to be of critical significance. But before I introduce an analytical framework based on aspects of their conceptual worlds, let me explore how the work- and author-concepts have been contested (or not) in contemporary musicology, and how the new critical approaches relate to the literary authorship theories developed in the previous section, examining what remains to be done.

The work- and author-concepts revisited

Even if the musical work- and composer-concepts have been reexamined from different perspectives during the past few decades, the most specific and significant body of scholarly contributions to the matter has been made by (or against) musical ontologists, scholars working within the field of the philosophy of music that primarily deal with the metaphysical nature of musical works.[34] Other approaches, such as those exploring the potential consideration of music as language, the sociological analysis of music, the definition of meaning in music, or the diverse perspectives introduced by contemporary composers in their writings have tended to deal with either seminal concepts tangentially.[35] As we shall see, confusion often arises in the ontological readings between two questions that are treated as quasi-identical: what is music? Versus what is the musical work?[36] Furthermore, most "traditional" ontological perspectives have generally abandoned the focus on the intention/meaning dualism that permeated literary approaches, favoring instead a focus on the identity, categorization, and legitimation issues.[37] Their central concern, a definition of the musical work, demotes and obscures the consideration of authorship, which emerges either as a lesser reflection or remains fully unquestioned.

The examples considered here, which represent an overview of the scholarship on the matter since the 1950s, have been divided into five main chronologically organized groups, based on the standard categories currently used by critics,[38] according to their significant commonalities: (1) traditionalist or realist orthodox views; (2) revisionist or realist unorthodox views; (3) those included in the "ontological turn" category; (4) the differing antirealist views; and (5) alternative approaches. An overall summary, which can be used as a general guide to the ensuing discussions, can be found in Table 2.2 and in Figures 2.1 and 2.2 (all included in the final Annex).[39]

The rationale that justifies my focus on these ontological readings is twofold: first, they introduce a survey of recent scholarship representative of the dominant views of the work- and author-concepts that permeate most contemporary musicology, resonate in music-teaching institutions, and shape our approach to music as performers; second, they provide a body of scholarly work that elucidates why I believe that a reconsideration of both concepts is necessary and how it might be undertaken from a poststructuralist-influenced perspective. The spotlight placed on the ontological readings is thus as partial as it is logical and practical, given the book's overall line of argument, the fact that it is not its core concern, and the impossibility of tracing a broader reading in such a limited space. The different ontological approaches will be considered individually, even if previous research has introduced well articulated and enlightening summaries, in order to highlight both their argumentative details and the nature of the chronological development that I attempt to portray.[40] My overall analytical hypothesis is that the work-concept(s) outlined by most ontological readings, which are embedded in the same philosophical tradition that made possible its emergence as a modern regulative notion, lead to a linear understanding of the work–composer relationship and to a prevalent theological vision of the composer as the Romantic individual god-author, as a creative demiurge, a vision that the . . . *Bach* . . . project seeks to contest. The laborious specificity of the ontological considerations and the brief remarks on their potential connections with recent developments in literary authorship theories provide the material for an examination of their underpinning assumptions. The need to challenge and transcend those premises will become clearer, in a retrospective gaze, as we reach the section's concluding lines.

Orthodox realists

Traditionalist or orthodox realist views are grounded on an acceptance of the existence of musical works as abstract ontological entities. Orthodox realists can be divided between those that follow a Nominalist approach, arguing that musical works "are collections of concrete particulars, such as scores and performances," and a Platonist approach, claiming that musical works are purely abstract objects (Kania 2016). Most Platonist approaches are permeated by a vision of works as *types*, that is, "generic entities which can have other entities [*tokens*] falling under them" (Davies 2011: 29). As a result, the categorization of musical work-types and the resultant conditions of instantiation of the work's tokens become key areas of discussion. Platonists can be further divided amid "simple" Platonists, those who understand works as eternal existents outside time and space, and "complex" Platonists, who claim that works come into existence as the products of human action. On the other hand, Nominalists can be divided between "class" Nominalists, who define works as the class formed by the set of compliant performances of a score, and "mereological" Nominalists, who envision works as fusions or sets of concrete objects.

A first significant historical referent is the analytical approach modeled on the proto-Nominalist work of Nelson Goodman (1906–1998), what David Davies labels the "Goodman argument," which had an impact on music in the critical writings of Jerrold Levinson (b. 1948), Peter Kivy (b. 1934), and Stephen Davies (b. 1950) – amongst others.[41] Goodman looks at notation as the source of answers for questions of musical ontology. He argues, following a strict identity criterion, that:

> the innocent-seeming principle that performances differing by just one note are instances of the same work risks the consequence – in view of the transitivity of identity – that all performances whatever are of the same work. If we allow the least deviation, all assurance of work-preservation and score-preservation is lost.
>
> (Goodman 1976: 187)

To put it differently, the score must "define a work," becoming the sole grantor of work-compliance conditions, while it must also be "uniquely determined" by each of its instances, being uniquely retrievable in each of them (Ibid.: 128 and 130). Goodman's perspective parallels the phenomenological belief in objective meanings, eliminating the need to discuss individual or internal intentions. In the absence of a theory of subjective creation, through the disengagement between the work and its history-of-production, the Romantic vision of the author as genius slips in, it becomes magical and is consequently reified. Furthermore, the fetishized centrality of the score as the only referent for the quasi-theological consideration of the work's identity reflects a Romantic vision of the composer as a god-creator.

A critical question arises when we accept that, as *types*, musical works are abstract entities that exist outside of time and space: how can they come into being? Jerrold Levinson introduces a first tentative answer, through a form of "qualified" or "complex" Platonism that confines its inquiry to the work-paradigm corresponding to the Western fully notated "classical" composition. Levinson articulates a vision of musical works as "initiated types," that is, not just sound structures *per se* but sound structures indicated by and indicative of a composer's intentionality: a sound structure-as-indicated-by-a-composer-at-a-time. The American philosopher argues that we should view composers as true creators because:

> It is one of the most firmly entrenched of our beliefs concerning art . . . the whole tradition of art assumes art is creative in the strict sense, that it is a godlike activity in which the artist brings into being what did not exist beforehand – much as a demiurge forms a world out of inchoate matter . . . if it is possible to align musical works with indisputably creatable artworks such as paintings and sculptures, then it seems we should do so . . . some of the status, significance, and value we attach to musical composition derives from our belief in this . . . there is a special glow that envelops composers, as well as other artists, because we think of them as true creators.
>
> (Levinson 1980: 8–9)

In Levinson's view, three key features account for the definition of musical works: (1) that they do not precede compositional activity (*creatability*), (2) that they are determined by musical-historical contexts (*fine individuation*), and (3) that specific means of performance or sound production are integral to them (*inclusion of performing means*).[42] Following this line of argument, Levinson points out that one of the essential elements involved in art making is the "'I–Thou' relation we take to exist between artist and work, a relation of unique possession. If works are to *belong* to artists in the full sense – to be theirs in no uncertain terms – then creation rather than discovery seems to be called for" (Levinson 2011: 218). Levinson's "qualified" Platonism conceives musical works as abstract indicated sound structures, while accepting the "author" as an "entrenched belief," one that does not need to be questioned. Although the possibility of a reassessment of the dominant work- and author-concepts is never considered, Levinson's reading introduces a key contribution through its "contextualism," a move that arguably parallels Foucault's interest in a historically situated understanding of the text, envisioning:

> [a]rtworks as essentially historically embedded objects, ones that have neither art status, nor determinate identity, nor clear aesthetic properties, nor definite aesthetic meanings, outside or apart from the generative contexts in which they arise and in which they are proffered.
>
> (Levinson 2007: 4)[43]

A different answer to the question of creatability is advanced by Peter Kivy, who, unlike Levinson, follows a "hard" or "simple" Platonist approach to argue that works are norm-types, abstract, and eternal individual objects that, as such, are discovered rather than created. The significance of artistic creativity or inspiration can be linked here to a vision of compositional "discovery . . . [as] invention, or creation" (Kivy 1993: 40). Kivy defines the performer as an "artist, somewhat akin to a composer or, better, 'arranger' of musical works" (Kivy 1995: 261). Interestingly, the American musicologist denies that "disputes over authorship, or changes in attribution" might have an impact on work-identity conditions (Kivy 1987: 247). Instead, intuition and musical common sense become key work-identity guarantors to articulate a reading in which music's most genuine or "real" dimension is our idea of it.[44] Kivy adopts Randall D. Dipert's model of multilayered compositional intentionality to stress that the composer's intentions, even if not fully realizable, "not only *do* play a major role [in our conception of music and performance] but *ought to* [do so]" (Kivy 1993: 96).[45] Hence, the score has to be respected as a source of testamental intentionality, one that might nonetheless be reinterpreted. Kivy's model stems from a form of metaphysical essentialism that is markedly work-centered and leads to an immaterial view of the work-concept, defined by Michael Gallope as the "musical work *qua* idea," that seems to be at odds with music's empirical and performative core (Gallope 2008: 95). Nonetheless, even if authorship emerges as a lesser reflection articulated as a theoretical necessity, Kivy partially counters, through the Platonic conception of compositional discovery, the Romantic theological vision of the author as a creator *ex nihilo*. Kivy's discussion of intentionality, linked to the simple Platonist view of creativity as a form of discovery, remains connected to the phenomenological exploration of the authorial meaning/intention dualism but introduces nuances that might be linked to Eco's interpretative intentionality or to Booth's discussion of implied authorship.

An earlier discussion of the abstractness of musical works and the issue of creatability, which can be connected to Levinson's "complex" Platonist approach, can be found in the writings of the Polish philosopher Roman Ingarden (1893–1970), particularly in his books *The Work of Music and the Problem of Its Identity* (1966) and *Ontology of the Work of Art: The Musical Work, the Picture, the Architectural Work, the Film* (1962), first published in English in 1986 and 1989, respectively. Ingarden defines the work as "a purely intentional object, immutable and permanent, whose heteronomous existence is no more than a reflection of its being: the existence of the work finds its source in the creative act of the performer, and its foundation in the score" (Nattiez 1990: 69). Intentional objects are thus different from "ideal" and "real" objects in that they are abstract yet located in time, can be created and destroyed, and depend for their "existence on conscious minds and upon real objects from which . . . [their] presence can be abstracted or inferred" (Davies 1988: 170). From this perspective, the score becomes a scheme that grants a flexibility upon which the work might be realized: "it is concomitant of its pure intentionality of the musical work that it has, so to speak, different foundations of its being and its appearing" (Ingarden 1989: 117). Ingarden has a unique conception of the work as a collaborative enterprise that emerges through the notion of "concretion":

> The *concretion* of the work is not only the reconstruction thanks to the activity of an observer of what was effectively present in the work, but also a completion of the work and the actualization of its moment of potentiality. It is thus in a way the common product of artist and observer.
>
> (Ingarden 1964: 199)

Pure intentionality plays a crucial role in Ingarden's view, which stresses both the possibility of an objective quasi-phenomenological meaning and the foundational centrality of the score while introducing – through the notion of "concretion" – a collaborative understanding of the work-concept that parallels the significance of the reader in the Derridean understanding of authorship.

Ingarden's argument over the heteronomous existence of musical works points toward a key aspect of the work's ontology that has not been considered so far: its social dimension. It is from this perspective that Nicholas Wolterstoff's (b. 1932) "simple" Platonist approach takes the traditional work-concept as a point of departure to posit an analytical shift toward its consideration as a socially charged reality, focusing on the social practices of art. He claims that "artists allow social realities to guide . . . [their] compositions, doing this in such a way that those realities become embodied in the works" (Wolterstoff in Alperson 1987: 108–109). Even if rules of correctness and rules of completeness are necessary to ground the existence of musical works, the traditional ontological focus on the works as isolated entities "must be expanded to embrace an ontology of practices" (Ibid.: 119). Works of music should thus be considered as "norm-kinds" of performances or "sound-sequence-occurrences."[46] However, Wolterstoff points out that "the basic reality of music is not the work nor the composition of works but music-making . . . [T]he composition of works is principally for the sake of enhancing a society's music making" (Ibid.: 121). Hence, the nature of musical works cannot be reduced to that of mere sound-patterns: music is not a sheer art of sounds but an art of sounds and actions (Ibid.: 125). What would then be the relationship between the work and the author/composer? Wolterstoff stresses that "the rationality of a work of art is neither purely interior to the work nor purely interior to the artist; not even its identity is" (Ibid.). Nonetheless, he argues that the evanescent nature of music and its works was only guaranteed by the development and employment of adequate notation and the subsequent solidity of the score. Furthermore, from Wolterstoff's perspective, the composer is not a "creator" but a "selector" of sound-patterns, patterns that, once set, become normative criteria: "the composer selects properties of sounds for the purpose of their serving as criteria for judging correctness of occurrence" (Wolterstoff 1980: 62). Wolterstoff introduces the idea of analogical predication as well in order to clarify the workings of the type/token model. If we distinguish between predicate and property sharing, we might argue that types – as eternal existents – possess properties that are only analogically evident in their performances – as specific events, works thus becoming only analogically perceivable. Even if some aspects of Wolterstoff's approach seem to parallel Foucault's stress on the relevance of contextualization, his terminological choices – rationality, identity, solidity of scores – and the quasi-phenomenological understanding of authorial intentionality as conveyed through the score, linked to Kivy's reading, showcase an openly traditionalist standpoint. The dominant idea of individual Romantic authorship remains here, once again, unchallenged.

Through the ontological analysis of the social dimension of music and its social practices, theorists have come to realize that the criteria for ontological categorization should be flexible if it aims to accommodate different historical and sociocultural realities. Such an approach has led Stephen Davies to explore a "complex" Platonist line, influenced by Levinson's reading, that proposes a mutable vision of the work as ontologically thinner or thicker – what he terms "ontological types" – depending on the amount of properties that one might consider constitutive within a given sociocultural reality and at a specific historical time (Davies 2008: 363–375). Davies argues that:

> the totality of musical works from culture to culture and from time to time do not have any single ontological character. Some musical works are thick with properties, other are thinner – some works include the performance-means as part of their essential nature, and much more besides, while others are more or less pure sound structures.
>
> (Davies 1991: 37)[47]

Against the Nominalist perspective, Davies stresses that the characteristics of the works-as-such are necessarily different from the characteristic of their instances (Davies in Levinson 2003: 155–180). He points out the impossibility of dealing with artistic enterprises through a "non-work-language" and thus the inescapability of the concept itself. Nonetheless:

> [b]ecause musical works are human creations, the sociology and psychology of music – what composers intend, what musicians do, and what listeners prefer, along with the interpersonal arrangements that emerge from or are based on such intentions, actions, and preferences – are relevant to an account of the character of the musical works that are made. Consideration of such matters is not . . . a turning away from metaphysics. It is, instead, the adoption of a metaphysics that is appropriately informed by relevant data from social and musical history.
> (Davies 2008: 373)

Regarding the significance of authorial intentionality, Davies claims that it should not determine our aesthetic understanding and appreciation of the composer's work. Authorial intentionality as conveyed in the score should be seen instead as a set of recommendations since "our aesthetic interest focuses upon the meanings which legitimately and coherently the work will sustain, rather than upon that which the author is able or prepared to avow as the meaning which he wished to communicate" (Davies 1982: 66). While Davies's approach does not question the centrality and/or validity of the work-concept, it does introduce a number of significant critical shadings: it stresses the need to avoid metaphysical essentialism, the significance of contextualization – which could arguably be seen as a Foucaldian element – and a vision of intentionality as a form of cooperation with the author's original gesture or "recommendation" that is reminiscent of Umberto Eco's authorial theories.

Davies's revisionist attitude might be historically symptomatic, but it is not predominant: harder traditionalist approaches are extremely influential still. An example can be found in the work of the English scholar Roger Scruton (b. 1944), who acknowledges the critical reading of the work-concept introduced by Lydia Goehr, Edward Said, and Carl Dahlhaus but argues that as a matter of fact we "*do* identify musical works, and identify them as particular objects of aesthetic interest" (Scruton 1997: 98). Scruton points out the centrality of the notion of numerical identity and attempts to adapt it to a musicological discussion.[48] In his view, the work is an immaterial and intentional object of perception that can be identified only through the use of metaphors. Scruton tellingly attempts to trace a parallelism with the ontology of paintings, arguing that:

> To identify the work of music in the material world is to identify the sound pattern intended by the composer, which is realized in performance by producing sound events. This sound pattern defines the

> salient features of the musical work, and can be written down in the form of a score.
>
> (Ibid.: 109)

The English philosopher adopts a pure sonicist perspective to posit that "the salient features of a musical work . . . are those which contribute to its tonal organization" (Ibid.: 110).[49] The musical work exists in "the habit of its reproduction," and a performance becomes "an attempt to determine the intentional object of a musical experience, by realizing the salient features of a sound pattern" (Ibid.: 112 and 110). Scruton's comparison with the ontology of painting unconsciously reveals the spurious origins of the application of the modern work-concept to music (see Goehr 2007: 149–151). The notion is not contested, though, and the intentionalist view retains its centrality.

Scruton is not alone in his continuation of the traditionalist readings. Julian Dodd, following Kivy's and Wolterstoff's orthodox Platonist model, introduces an approach termed the "simple view" that conceives musical works as uncreatable but discoverable eternal norm-types. Musical works *qua* norm-types are "*essentially instantiable* even though they exist when uninstantiated" and their tokens are "datable, locatable patterns of sound, sound-sequence events" (Dodd 2007: 107 and 3). Therefore, the role of the author/composer, following the Platonist readings, is not that of a creator but a discoverer of preexisting sonic entities. Dodd holds, countering Scruton's pure sonicist approach, a "timbral sonicist" view, arguing that the employment of the indicated instruments or the historical contextualization of a score/performance cannot be considered as part of a musical work's identity criteria. Furthermore, Dodd claims that "what is essential to composition is *creativity*, not the creation of an entity" (Dodd 2000: 427).[50] Composition thus becomes a kind of "creative discovery" and the musical work the indicating or instantiating of a structure, "the action of prescribing certain things for correct performance" (Davies 2011: 43). Dodd's reading expands here the "simple" Platonist view, as a result, the vision of musical works as abstract eternal structures and the secondary role of authorship, as in Kivy's example, remain pivotal and undisputed.

As I pointed out earlier, these Platonist approaches need to be seen as a reaction against Goodman's early proto-Nominalism, which had a deep influence on the subsequent ontological considerations of the musical work during the second half of the twentieth century. Furthermore, Goodman's class Nominalism was eventually complemented by new mereological approaches like those found in Chris Tillman's Endurantist perspective. Tillman's reading can be defined as that of a musical materialist that rejects any form of abstractionism. Musical works are consequently conceived as material rather than abstract objects, avoiding the Platonist "perennial temptation" (Tillman 2011: 14). Endurantists argue that the concrete manifestations of a work, called "musical atoms," do not bear a relationship of parthood to the work – as on Nominalist perdurantism – but are characterized instead by a permanent overlap: "a musical work is multiply located and occupies any region exactly occupied by any of its musical atoms" (Ibid.: 19). Yet, while being wholly located at any space occupied by their atoms, musical works are not identical to them. Tillman's discussion does not include a consideration of authorship; it is instead a work-centered metaphysically essentialist reading that by ignoring, like Goodman, the significance of subjective creation, implicitly accepts a Romantic reification of the author. The dominant conceptual framework is not challenged.

Unorthodox realists

We have explored so far different realist orthodox views, those in which the modern work-concept and Romantic authorship remain typically unquestioned. The present section explores instead various revisionist or unorthodox realist approaches, readings that, while accepting the existence of musical works, introduce alternative standpoints to counter some of the dominant ideas permeating the traditional Platonist and Nominalist arguments. An early significant example can be found in the writings of the German musicologist Carl Dahlhaus (1928–1989). In the opening chapter of his unfinished book, *Die Musiktheorie im 18. und 19. Jahrhundert*, Dahlhaus introduced a definition of the Romantic or modern work-concept through four key constituent yet problematic characteristics: (1) originality, (2) canonic status, (3) organic wholeness, and (4) aesthetic autonomy (Dahlhaus *et al.* 1984: 30–31). The German theorist contested the role of the score as the work's grounding element, defining the musical work as a text located beside either its notated form or any acoustic rendering bonded by an explicit or implicit "intentional element" (Dahlhaus *et al.* 1982: 94).[51] According to Dahlhaus, the hermeneutic understanding-process necessarily becomes part of what the work is, the analytical framework being critically internalized (Ibid.: 95). Dahlhaus's challenge to the previously dominant notion of intentionality arguably parallels elements of Foucaldian theory, linked to the "author-function" and the significance of contextualization, as well as aspects of New Historicism, related to the consideration of the author and the work as textually and socio-historically embedded realities. Furthermore, Dahlhaus's approach markedly influenced Goehr's historicist perspective since it grounded and opened up the possibility of a thorough reassessment of authorship and workhood, even if it failed to fully articulate an alternative paradigm.

However, Dahlhaus's unorthodox realism would not be the only reading to introduce a valuable and influential critique of the traditional concepts.

Peter Lamarque (b. 1948) posited a different revisionist approach on an article entitled "Work and Object," articulating a distinct reexamination of the traditional discourses. Lamarque's type of class Nominalism might be conservative in its consideration of workhood, but it does nonetheless advance some key novelties that counter the traditionalist approach through its examination of authorship. Lamarque argues that works of art have:

> [r]eal, not ideal identities (they do not exist only in the minds of those who contemplate them); they are public and perceivable . . .; they possess their properties objectively, some essential, some inessential; they are cultural objects, dependent for their inception and survival on cultural conditions; more specifically, they are entities essentially tied to human acts and attitudes; they are created, for example, by artists; they can come into and go out of existence . . .; and their identity conditions, being value-laden, are distinct from those of functionally defined artefacts and physical objects in the natural world.
>
> (Lamarque 2002: 146)[52]

With the regard to the work/author relationship, Lamarque points out that "when the (artist's) work stops the work (of art) starts. Indeed it seems a necessary condition for a work to come into existence that the work on it has been completed" (Lamarque in Krausz *et al.* 2009: 105). Lamarque establishes a difference between "aesthetic completion," the outcome of aesthetic analysis, and "genetic completion," resulting from the creator's own conscious act of closure, two dimensions that might not be necessarily coincident. Yet completion cannot be conceived as taking place against a cultural vacuum: it is instead a historically, culturally, and institutionally mediated act that requires the artist's intention to create the kind of work that she/he is actually creating. Although Lamarque focuses on the ontology of works of art in general, his ideas can also be applied to the consideration of musical works. His approach arguably parallels Pareyson's view of the emergence of artistic intention from interpretative readings, since works depend on cultural conditions to be created and survive. Furthermore, Lamarque stands on the side of Nominalism to counter the traditional Platonist view of works as ideas rather than real entities and the understanding of authorship as creative discovery rather than as a form of pure creation. However, even if the text engages in a partial discussion of the conditions of authorship, the dominant notion seems to unconsciously underpin, once again, Lamarque's approach.

Lamarque's innovative class Nominalism can also be linked to David Davies's unorthodox reading, what has been referred to as the performative view of musical works, as developed in his books *Art as Performances* and *Philosophy of the Performing Arts* (Davies 2004, 2011). Davies critically adopts Gregory Currie's "action theory" to argue that, factually, musical works, which are defined as "multiple artworks" following Goodman's notion of allographic art,[53] emerge through performance: "it is part of the very concept of a performable work that it can be properly or fully *appreciated* through, and only through, performances" (Davies 2011: 25).[54] According to Davies, certain qualities of musical works "relevant to their being appreciated as the particular works that they are, are only realizable, and thereby made available to receivers, in . . . performances" (Davies 2009: 745) As a result, works are not conceptualized as the product of the artist's creative action but as the activity or process that brings about that product. Conceived as action-tokens or token performances rather than as ideal types, works reflect their greater similarity to "processes than to their products *simpliciter*" (Davies 1999: 150). Davies explains this further when he points out that an artwork "is a performance that specifies a focus of appreciation," comprising an "articulated content in a broad sense, a vehicle by means of which the content is articulated, and a set of shared understandings – an 'artistic medium' – which mediates between the vehicle and the content" (Davies 2004: 146). Such a processual vision of the work reintroduces the significance of authorial semantic intentions, related to the composer's employment of the vehicular medium, upon the work's evaluation and appreciation. Nonetheless, Davies's reading, in spite of its powerful critique of some of the key traditional ontological assumptions, leads to a vision of the linkage between the composer's mind and her/his object of creation that remains teleologically linear. Davies's adoption of the action-token idea might be linked to the centrality of the reader in the Derridean model or to Foucault's vision of the author as a variable function of discourse, but his liminal argument lingers on the confining space of essentialist musical metaphysics.

A different critique of the type/token relationship as a model for the consideration of the ontological status of repeatable works has been introduced by Guy Rohrbaugh (b. 1968). Against their consideration as types, Rohrbaugh proposes an alternative three-level model on which all artworks share a modal flexibility – "they could have had qualities other than they actually do," a temporal flexibility – "they are susceptible to change in their qualities over time," and are determined by their temporality – "they come into and go out of existence" (Rohrbaugh 2003: 178). Works of art and works of music are not identical to ideal structures but become instead historically determined: they are "objects in and persisting through history, ones which merely have a certain form" (Ibid.). Musical works are thus envisioned as "continuants," higher-order historical individuals that depend for their existence on their specific embodiments. Rohrbaugh points out that a "properly conceived ontology of art is one which provides a metaphysical framework flexible enough to represent accurately a wide variety of phenomena and to permit the expression of heterogeneous critical views" (Ibid.). Against the unstable and ill suited universal/particular terminology, Rohrbaugh defines photographies and, by extension other repeatable artworks, as "non-physical historical individuals, continuants which stand in a relation of ontological dependence to a casually connected series of physical (sometimes mental) particulars," particulars that include both instances and occurrences (Ibid.: 198). Rohrbaugh's reading, which introduces a form of endurantism in which works depend upon but are not comprised by their manifestations, posits an interesting challenge to the dominant work- and author-concepts through an approach that could be linked to the Foucaldian author-function and the resultant vision of the text as emerging from an interface of other texts. The composer–work relationship and the traditional author-concept remain nonetheless unchallenged.

The ontological turn

During the final decades of the twentieth century, the new compositional and experiential realities of the musical avant-garde have called for a revision of the traditional ontological assumptions. European scholars Alessandro Arbo (b. 1963) and Marcello Ruta have endorsed an ontological turn in continental musicology. Their vision can be framed in the larger new analytical approach articulated by the "ontological turn" movement that emerged in the 1980s as a reaction to the "semiotic turn" of the 1970s and the "writing culture" of the 1980s. This new form of anthropological ontology abandoned the previous focus on the "discursive aspects of cultural representation" and favored the consideration of culture as representation (Clifford and Marcus 1986: 13). Arbo and Ruta stress the significance of the movement's historical background to explain that the current emergence of a new musical ontology stems from the "orientation of contemporary philosophical thought, more and more marked by the so-called ontological turn, after the renowned period of reflection on language and symbolic systems" (Arbo and Ruta 2014: 5). Nicolo Palazzetti explains this further by pointing out that "the renaissance of the ontology of music is an attempt to enable musicological research to deal with contemporary musical practices, informed by globalization, cultural pluralism, and the affirmation of the Computer Age in the wake of the Digital Revolution" (Palazzetti 2015: 191). One of Ruta's most interesting remarks is articulated against the commonsensical acceptance of both the work-concept and creation and artistic endeavor "as *creation ex nihilo* . . . [that is] bringing into existence something that was not there before" – as introduced by Levinson (Ruta 2014). Regarding the first element, Ruta stresses that, by looking both at the existing literature on the subject and at musical examples outside the Western classical tradition, we realize that the idea of a musical work is not univocal or evident and that, as a result, it should be understood as a historically shifting category. With regard to the traditional understanding of creation, Ruta points out that even "by limiting ourselves to the western civilization . . . the idea of artistic creation is quite a young one," one that emerges from a Romantic reading of Platonic philosophy (Ibid.). Ruta introduces here, within the novel focus put forward by the "ontological turn," a valuable critique of the traditional realist views that has many elements in common with my own rationale and approach. Nonetheless, his reading remains ontological, positing a critical reading of creativeness and authorship that is not fully compatible, as we shall see, with that permeating the . . . *Bach* . . . project and this book's overall line of argument.

Antirealists

Antirealists, those theorists who deny the existence of musical works or question the validity of the modern work-concept and its ontological examination, can be divided into five main categories.[55] First, we find "historicists," such as Lydia Goehr, who challenge the very nature of the unhistorical approach permeating the field of musical ontology. Second, "semanticists" like Amie Thomasson argue that metaphysical disputes on music and art can be reduced to a verbal matter, one that should be approached semantically through the exploration of the different meanings that are attributed to different analytical concepts. On the other hand, we have "aesthetic dismissivists" such as Aaron Ridley, who adopt the aestheticist paradigm to stress the value of an aesthetic approach to musical works against meaningless ontological readings.[56] A further antirealist view can be found on the work of "eliminativists" like Ross Cameron, who dismisses the work-concept *tout court* arguing that the evidence of their existence does not constitute an ontological fact; it does not make them ontologically "real." Finally, "fictionalists" such as Robert Kraut argue that an ontological approach to music is unnecessary since it does not complement our understanding of musical works as articulated in musicological or music-theoretical discourses.

The work of Richard Rudner (1921–1979) represents an early example of an antirealist approach. Rudner questioned the metaphysical divide that differentiates abstract from concrete music. His standpoint stressed that the occurrence of the name of the artwork is a "syncategorematic one," arguing that the term has no real meaning when standing on itself and that it cannot consequently serve as the subject or the predicate of a proposition. This very fact "confers a certain plausibility on the decision that their designata are abstract entities" (Rudner 1950: 386). From Rudner's perspective, the abstractness of musical works denies their experiential accessibility. As a result, musical works should not be considered as anything besides their performances, an argument in line with David Davie's performative view. Rudner's critical reading combines the Barthesian centrality of the reader/performer, one linked to the "birth of the reader/death of the author" dualism, and Pareyson's vision of intention as essentially articulated through interpretative readings.

A different antirealist perspective can be found in the work of the American musicologist Lydia Goehr (b. 1960). As we have seen, Goehr introduces a "historicist" approach that articulates a critical vision of workhood stemming from a cultural and historical analysis of its emergence. Goehr defines works as open concepts, concepts that do not require specification of boundary conditions.[57] Open concepts require instead "a sense of continuity or tradition . . . [They] can be expanded and modified over time as new examples become paradigmatic . . . [T]heir definitions might be altered . . . [and] might be treated as open for some purposes and closed for others" (Lutterman 2006: 45). This conceptual framework leads to an understanding of the dominant work-concept as regulative rather than constitutive, one that guides "the practice externally by indicating the point of following the constitutive rules" (Goehr 2007: 102). From such a perspective, the work-concept is also defined as projective, since "works do not exist other than in projected form; what exists is the regulative work-concept" and emergent, since it might crystallize at a particular historical moment even if "many if not all the threads of what becomes the concept already exist [prior to its emergence]. As yet, however they are not meshed together in the appropriate way to admit the concept's regulative function" (Ibid.: 106 and 108). Although Goehr does not fully articulate an alternative model, the dominant view of the authoriality remaining consequently uncontested, her historicist approach arguably parallels elements of Foucaldian theory in its exploration of the process of emergence of the intentional and the textual and in the significance given to the historical and cultural contextualization of literary works and authors. Furthermore, Goehr's critical perspective has had a fundamental impact on contemporary musicology, making possible and facilitating the emergence of new paradigms and approaches, such as the one advanced in this book.

One of the most salient aspects of Goehr's analysis is its stress on the significance that our awareness of a concept's historicity should have in any critical attempt to understand its current or dominant usage and bearing. A similar critique can be found in Amie Thomasson's (b. 1968) "semanticist" reading, which explores how the underpinning verbal and conceptual dimensions shape most ontological discussions and their implied foundational assumptions. Thomasson criticizes the "discovery view" approach to musical ontology, pointing out that "knowledge claims in the ontology of art are often presented as discoveries of fully determinate, mind-independent facts about the ontological status of works of art of various kinds, about which everyone may be ignorant or in error" (Thomasson 2005: 221). The American philosopher stresses the need for a meta-ontological critique of ontological discourses, pointing out that "the ontology of the work of art must be something we learn about through conceptual analysis of the associated concepts of people who competently ground . . . the reference of terms like 'symphony' and 'painting,' not something we can seek to *discover* through investigations into mind-independent reality" (Ibid.: 223). According to Thomasson, a valid criterion to determine the inclusion in a given art-kind is the artist's intention to create a work of that given sort based on a background conception of "what *ontological* sort of art-kind he/she means the term to refer to, establishing existence conditions and identity conditions for works of that kind" (Ibid.: 225). Consequently, the traditional approaches to art ontology have to be abandoned in favor of a meta-critique or conceptual analysis of their tacit underlying ontological premises. Thomasson's meta-critique, if we observe the previously explored literary perspective, combines elements of Foucault's vision of the subject/author as a cultural product and the sociohistorical and textualized vision of the author introduced by the New Historicists. Nonetheless, her approach, while positing a valuable critique of the traditional readings, remains meta-ontological and does not engage in a direct discussion of the work- and author-concepts, which are not actually contested.[58]

Thomasson's meta-ontological review does not manage to transcend metaphysical essentialism, but it stresses the necessity to question the nature of our analytical and conceptual assumptions. Her argument can be further stretched, following Aaron Ridley's (b. 1962) "dismissivist" perspective, to counter the very possibility and value of a musical ontology. Ridley points out that "a serious philosophical engagement with music is orthogonal to, and may well in fact be impeded by, the pursuit of ontological issues" (Ridley 2003: 203). From Ridley's aestheticist approach, the ontological discussions are musically meaningless. While the ontological focus is placed on performance and work-legitimation, musicological research should be centered on aesthetic qualitative examination, on evaluative issues, establishing a distinction between a philosophical and a critical interest in music. Ridley believes that a definition of what a work is does not necessarily have to precede a definition of its aesthetic value and that the nature of both debates should remain completely distinct. Even if Ridley envisions traditional musical ontological discussions as the outcome of both the "lure of meta-physics" and the "unwittingly baleful influence of Nelson Goodman" (Ridley 2004: 121), his antirealist view has been criticized by music ontologists who argue that it is in fact permeated by the same ontological assumptions that he attempts to reject (Kania 2008: 70). In any case, Ridley's critique of what he terms the "autonomaniac view" – the view that music is a "quasi-syntactical structure of sound understandable solely in musical terms . . . and making no reference to anything beyond itself" – can be linked to elements that grounded the conception of the . . . *Bach* . . . project and this book's overall argument and methodological approach (Ridley 2004: 166). Although the significance of both the internal and external (intrinsic/extrinsic) understandings of music can be arguably connected to Barthesian analytical plurality, Ridley's reading fails to introduce an alternative model, one that might serve to critically rearticulate the traditional understanding of the author-concept.

In spite of its common interest in the need to reconsider our basic analytic and intellectual premises, Ridley's approach represents a radical departure from all the antirealist readings explored so far. However, the aestheticist paradigm has been outweighed by the abundance of meta-ontological critiques. A case in point can be found in the work and writings of Ross Cameron. Cameron's "eliminitavism" is grounded in the assumption that, from a meta-ontological perspective, the affirmation that "*a* exists can be true without committing us to an entity that is *a*" (Cameron 2008: 295). The Scottish philosopher traces a divide between the nature of a true statement in common English and in what he terms as *Ontologese*, "the language we use to describe how the world is at its fundamental level," following what has been defined as the "paraphrasing strategy" (Ibid.: 300–301). He summarizes his view on the following terms: instead of works, "all there is . . . is a collection of (enduring) simples, arranged a certain way for a while, and then arranged a different way as the result of the intentional action of agents" (Ibid.: 298–299). Cameron's perspective is that of a compositional and musical nihilist, someone who denies mereological parthood.[59] The key question stops being what the musical work is or might be and becomes what must the world be like for it to make the case that musical works actually exist. Cameron's answer is that "all that has to happen is that some of the eternally existing abstract sound structures [have to] get indicated by composers, who lay down instruction for their performance" (Ibid.: 305–306). Composers thus create by letting preexisting sound structures perform a role as a musical work, an argument that parallels the "simple" Platonist view of artistic creativity. This raises an issue that Cameron leaves unanswered, that of the composer's *epistemic access* to abstract sound structures. Despite its meta-ontological critique, Cameron's reading of the work- and author-concepts, which seems to be permeated by Umberto Eco's idea of openness and his dual vision of authorial intentionality, does not ultimately posit a direct or real challenge to the dominant readings, remaining very closely connected to the paradigms explored earlier in the consideration of the realist standpoints.[60]

The need to explore the assumptions that ground most approaches to the ontological consideration of the musical work and musical authorship, exemplified by Thomasson's and Cameron's meta-ontological arguments, has also been followed by Robert Kraut (b. 1946) in his antirealist "fictionalist" examination. Kraut proposes that "the foregrounding of explanation [as a scientific approach] when thinking about [art and music] ontology must be resisted" (Kraut 2012: 686). Explanations of artworks can be conceived only as explanations of human action, that is, as psychological explanations that might not conform to the standard scientific models. From Kraut's perspective, ontological discourses on music can be predominantly defined as attempts to justify or legitimize an already institutionalized intellectual practice. His reading is encapsulated in the following words:

> The artworld ontologist wishes to know *what kind of a thing an artwork is;* the music ontologist wishes to know *what kind of a thing a musical work is*. On one reasonable understanding of these goals, such knowledge is already provided by critics, historians, musicologists, and consumers of art.
>
> (Ibid.: 707)

Kraut argues that the key problem with ontological discussions is that "talk of universals provides neither explanation nor justification for our classifications, but serves . . . as a mechanism for making the correctness of such classifications. That correctness, in turn, is grounded in linguistic normativities rather than shared entities" (Kraut 2010: 596).[61] Kraut's "fictionalism" introduces a powerful antirealist critique of the methodologies that permeate traditional musical ontologies. His view remains nonetheless meta-ontological, like Thomasson's, and consequently avoids a direct discussion and/ or potential reformulation of the work- and author-concepts.

Alternative approaches

As I discussed in the opening lines of the present section, it would be misleading to suggest that the consideration of the work- and author-concepts in music has only been posited from purely onto-metaphysical perspectives, even if these represent the most abundant scholarly contribution to the matter. I will briefly discuss here some influential attempts to articulate different readings, readings that exemplify current paths of research based on alternative intellectual frameworks stemming from both filo-ontological and nonontological approaches.

A unique vision of the work- author-concepts emerges from Jean-Jacques Nattiez's (b. 1945) semiotic exploration. Nattiez disperses the work's being

Poietic process → Score → Musical Result ← Esthetic Process
↑
Interpretation
(performance)

Example 2.1 J. J. Nattiez, *Music and Discourse*, p. 73

among three distinct spheres: "in the interaction between its symbolic components, as a total musical fact; as poietic strategies, a resultant trace, and esthesic strategies unleashed by that trace" (Nattiez 1990: 70). The score thus becomes the object that "ensues from the composer's creative act," not a mere scheme but an essentially mnemonic device (Ibid.: 71). If the work emerges from the relations fixed by the score, the graphic sign *is* the work (poietic process), and the esthesic process begins with and follows its interpretation, which marks as well the end of the poietic process (see Example 2.1). Musical works are hence understood as a form of "allographic art": any interpretation that conveys an acceptable correspondence between graphic text and performance is considered authentic.[62] Interpretation, from this flexible approach, involves various symbolic forms and layers. Although based on the "traditional" model, Nattiez's scheme (summarized in Example 2.1), somehow emulating the style of Barthes's multidimensional approach, seems to question the possibility of a single theological reading.

One further unconventional angle can be found in the work of Richard Littlefield, who shifts the focus from the consideration of the work itself to an exploration of its boundary conditions in an attempt to find out "what goes on at the borders of a musical work?" (Littlefield 1996: 1).[63] Littlefield filters and develops Edward T. Cone's view of silence as a framing element through the ideas of Jacques Derrida, as structured in his critique of Immanuel Kant's vision of the frame as mere ornament in the *Critique of Pure Judgment*. His argument leads him to the following conclusion:

> In "normal" music analysis and interpretation, musical silence, like the picture frame, tends to erase itself. In their role as crucial structural determinants . . . silences rarely figure into systematic accounts of the musical act, just as in the recollection of a novel, criticism usually does not go to spaces between lines, paragraphs, sections, and chapters.
>
> (Ibid.: 7)

Even if Littlefield seeks to approach the musical work from the outside, from its otherness, his critical use of Derridean models does not contest the classical paradigm and its associated author- and work-concepts. As a matter of fact, in the opening lines of his article, he points out that he takes for granted "the commonly accepted definition [of a musical work], at least since the Renaissance . . . [as] an 'opus perfectum et absolutum' – a finished man-made product, a self-sufficient entity sui generis that exists beyond the place and time of its creation" (Ibid.: 1).

Derrida's influential intellectuality has not been the sole source of inspiration igniting a reassessment of the dominant musical work- and author-concepts. Michael Gallope articulates a further critique of the traditional approach through an adaptation of the ideas of the French intellectual Gilles Deleuze. Gallope's proposal entails a radical revision of the musical work; he argues:

> Instead of expressing or representing something about socio-cultural identity, history, or a composer or performer, music would challenge, or "deterritoritalize" precisely these worldly, actual properties. What is musical about music is something that exceeds the boundaries of social formations. Music is really a flux of sensation that is so completely new from moment to moment that it reminds us that life is becoming new from moment to moment.
>
> (Gallope 2008: 101–102)

Furthermore:

> The flights of joyous and virtual music becoming proper to a Deleuzian work leave the discrete "symphony" behind, becoming nothing but sensations, flowing through players and listeners alike. These are sensations that, in themselves, forget their capacity to remain faithful to the musical form, to a composer's specific expression, to a historical epoch, or to any situation.
>
> (Ibid.: 102)

According to Gallope, Deleuze's philosophy dismantles the regulative power of those abstract ideas that permeate musicological and music-philosophical discourses by "refusing all moments of transcendent mediation" (Ibid.: 103). Through their negation of subjective and objective coordinates, Deleuzian musical works become self-founding or self-positing. Deleuze argues that art "is independent of the creator through the self-positing of the created, which is preserved in itself. What is preserved – the thing or the work of art – is *a bloc of sensations, that is to say, a compound of percepts and affects*" (Deleuze and Guattari 1994: 163–164). As a result, as Gallope points out, "music for him is based on a materiality of sound but is not reducible to any social or perceptual situation. It has a strange kind of autonomy, one that is oriented towards the absolute, but *not* as a vehicle for the actual work's content" (Gallope 2008: 117). The Deleuzian work thus "overcomes all its mediations, reproductions, and technical supports to expand the singularity of its sensation through a limitless assemblage of nervous systems"; the work of music becomes, from this perspective, a "singularity of cosmic power" (Ibid.: 118). Gallope's reading introduces a novel framework that, although based on a different intellectual background, shares many elements with my own critical approach: the work-concept might not be fully abandoned, but both the Romantic quasi-theological vision of the author and the traditional onto-metaphysical constraints are critically challenged.

Medial caesura

So, what conclusions might be reached from these detailed examinations? I believe that, beyond the valuable critiques posited by some of the antirealist and alternative approaches, most of the selective ontological considerations of the work- and author-concepts introduced thus far are permeated by two key assumptions, arguably derived from a shared essentialist metaphysical background.[64] First, the vast majority treats the "work of the composer as the main center of interest and as the *true aesthetic* object" (Giombini 2015: 186). Consequently, they rarely question the validity of either the idiom or the modern work-concept itself as a theoretical construct. Furthermore, since the attempts to undermine the traditional model do not fully articulate an alternative critical framework (i.e., Goehr, Ridley, Gallope), the work-concept remains essentially unchallenged. Secondly, the consideration of authorship does not play a central role and is often reduced to a simple linear equation: the author is, plainly, the subject that creates/discovers/unveils/indicates the musical work. Such a vision exposes the reduced impact that the approaches developed in literary theory during the past sixty years have had on these musicological discourses – with the only exceptions of the most daring antirealist (i.e., Thomasson and Cameron) and alternative (i.e., Littlefield and Gallope) views. In addition, nearly all the theorists that engage in an exploration of the relationships among the different elements that make possible the musical-work-game (composer, performer, audience, score, performance, etc.) treat them as closed and differentiated compartments, connected, if at all, by linkages reducible to logical formulations, thus ignoring their overlapping fluidity and the processual complexity of music. Is the matter really that simple? I believe that it is not.

My argument is that most of the ontological (or anti-ontological) examinations explored here emerge from and are trapped within a form of vicious circularity. Music theorists might reply that my attempt to trace a connection between the development of literary author/work theories and musicological discussions is unnecessary, artificial, or even distorting. But, given the common underpinning philosophical body upon which these ontological readings are built, such linkage, even if vaguely articulated, might prove to be an enlightening transdisciplinary exercise, one that could help us abandon such metaphysical inflexibility. In *The Truth in Painting*, Derrida introduces, amid a discussion and explication of Heideggerian ideas, the following argument that illustrates my point and is worth quoting in full:

> Why a circle? Here is the schema of the argument: to look for the origin of a thing is to look for that from which it starts out and whereby it is what it is, it is to look for its essential provenance, which is not its empirical origin. The work of art stems from the artist, so they say. But what is an artist? The one who produces works of art. The origin of the artist is the work of art, the origin of the work of art is the artist, "neither is without the other." Given this, "artist and work are in themselves and in their reciprocity (*Wechselbezug*) by virtue of a third term (*durch ein Drittes*) which is indeed the first, namely that from which artist and work of art also get their name, art." What is art? As long as one refuses to give an answer in advance to this question, "art" is only a word. And if one wants to interrogate art, one is indeed obliged to give oneself the guiding thread of a representation. And this thread is the work, the fact that there are works of art. Repetition of the Hegelian gesture in the necessity of its lemma: there are works which common opinion [*l'opinion courante*] designates as works of art and they are what one must interrogate in order to decipher in them the essence of art. But by what does one recognize, commonly [*courammen*t], that these are works of art if one does not have in advance a sort of precomprehension of the essence of art? This hermeneutic circle has only the (logical, formal, derived) appearance of a vicious circle.
>
> (Derrida 1987: 31–32)[65]

This ongoing *circulus in probando* needs to be brought to a halt: both its tacit assumptions and those fundamental aspects that remain unexplored need to be contested from new critical perspectives. A reexamination of the boundary between the aesthetic and metaphysical examinations of music is also necessary.[66] The reconsideration of musical textuality exemplified by the . . . *Bach* . . . project provides a powerful point of departure. It is in that light that, following my original argument, structuralist and post-structuralist thinking and, more precisely, Derrida's and Barthes's ideas, their understanding of authorship and of the literary text, will prove to be an important source of tools for critical scrutiny. The following chapter explores those elements as a necessary prelude/pre-text to the musical analyses – analytical dissections of the newly emerging extended-musical-textuality – introduced in the final chapter of the book.

Notes

1 For further reading, see Eagleton (1983), Burke (1995), and Waugh (2006).

2 Wimsatt's and Beardsley's notion of intentional fallacy implies that the design "or intention of the author is neither available nor desirable as a standard for judging the success of a work of literary art" (Wimsatt and Beardsley 1954: 3). This approach had been predated by the theories of the Italian writer and philosopher Benedetto Croce (Croce 1992).

3 Both Barthesian and Derridean theories will be explored in a greater detail in the ensuing sections of the text.

4 Andrew Bennet has criticized Barthes's reading of the romantic author, arguing that it overlooks and "misrepresents . . . the complexities and self-contradictions that energize Romantic poetic theory" (Waugh 2006: 57).

5 In *Signéponge/Signsponge*, Derrida writes with regard to the Barthesian idea of the "death of the author" that the nature of signature is "not inconsistent with that death or omission of the author of which, as is certainly the case, too much of a case has been made" (Derrida 1984: 22). For a further, more enlightening critique, see Derrida (2001: 49–59).

6 David Bates explains Derridean undecidability on the following terms:

> For Derrida, undecidability was never a synonym for mere indeterminacy, or some loose free play of meaning. Rather, undecidability was a way of explaining a very specific structural condition at the heart of language. Undecidability was what preceded and therefore made possible the production of any of the determinate meanings that then had to be "decided" for meaning to unfold in any particular reading.
>
> (Bates 2005: 4)

7 This is part of Foucault's influential article, "What Is an Author?" (Foucault 1984: 101–120).

8 See also Nancy K. Miller in Burke (1995: 193–211).

9 According to Bouveresse's critique of the "myth of interiority," it is illusory to believe that we can fully understand the meaning that a given sentence might have for the individual uttering it (Bouveresse 1976). For further reading on Wittgenstein's ideas, see Wittgenstein (2009).

10 For further reading, see Anscombe (2000).

11 For further reading, see Luigi Pareyson (2009: 161–190).

12 A key contribution in this regard has been Marcel Cobussen's dissertation, "Deconstruction in Music" (Cobussen 2002). Another important contribution, partially linked to Cobussen's arguments, has been made by Suzanne Palfy, who has explored the role and nature of musical agency as an intersubjective phenomenon (Palfy 2015).

13 Umberto Eco argues that music is a purely syntactic system with no apparent semantic depth. Music thus presents, on the one hand, "the problem of a semiotic

system without a semantic level (or a content pane); on the other hand, however, there are musical 'signs' (or syntagms) with an explicit denotative value . . . and there are syntagms or entire 'texts' containing pre-culturalized connotative value" (Eco 1979: 11). On the other hand, Roland Barthes refers to music as a second-order semiological system (Barthes 1972: 115). Henry Orlov goes even further to stress that:

> semiotics as a descriptive analytical method must be further refined and adjusted for it to become a useful and productive approach to the peculiarly complex system of music . . . for it seems somewhat improbable that a concept formed on the basis of linguistics should have an immediate explanatory power outside its original boundaries.
>
> (Steiner 1981: 132)

14 A reconsideration that has been partially undertaken, in any case, from a number of perspectives. A selective list of significant examples would include Claude Levi-Strauss (1969: 14–30), Pousseur (1972), Ruwet (1972), Stefani (1973), Osmond-Smith (1973), Steiner (1981), Nattiez (1990), Monelle (1992), Tarasti (1994), Merrell (1995), Almen (2008), Agawu (2009), and Sheinberg (2012).

15 I understand that this contention is difficult, if not impossible to prove. I am also aware of the fact that such notions of the work- and author-concepts might remain prominent in certain musicological fields, like those of music theory or in biographical studies, and have been more pertinently contested in others, like musical semiotics or music sociology. In any case, anyone with a broad acquaintance of recent musical scholarship would agree that a shift in how those notions determine most musicological research is still to be made.

16 Bennett points out that the Romantic author is seen as "originator and genius, as [a] fully intentional, fully sentient source of the literary text, as authority for and limitation on the 'proliferating' meanings of the text" (Bennet 2005: 55). Similarly, Goehr points out that Romantic composers were seen as divinely inspired creators with the authority to "express 'higher truths' within their works, an authority . . . regarded as contingent upon the composers' separation from the ordinary, every-day world" (Goehr 2007: 209). Let me stress here that the matter of the romantic vision of musical authorship, which goes beyond the scope of this book, is complex and historically fluid. For further reading, see Bent (1996), Leader (2000), Hunter (2005), and Neubauer (2009). A narrowly selective list of specific primary sources, which is not intended to be exhaustive but representative of some of the dominant views at the time, would include Hegel (1975: 888–958), Schumann (1988), Hoffmann (1989), Schelling (1989), Liszt (1999), and Marx (2009).

17 It is important to acknowledge that Goehr's approach is not completely novel: it was heavily influenced by the previous work of German scholars such as Carl Dahlhaus and other critics of modernism in the 1960s (as an example, see Dahlhaus 1989). The critiques and challenges raised against Goehr's arguments will be explored in the following section. For further reading on this matter, see Talbot (2000: 168–186) and Erauw (1998: 109–115).

18 Nikolai Listenius, born in Hamburg c. 1510, was one of the most important German theorists of the Renaissance (Listenius 1927). See also Goehr (2007: 116). A thorough consideration of the use of the work-concept by early German theorists can be found in Heinz von Loesch's *Der Werkbegriff in Der Protestantischen*

Musiktheorie Des 16. und 17. Jahrhunderts (Loesch 2001). Loesch shows that most sources evidence different understandings of the practice of music and links the emergence of the term to the development of Protestant theology in Northern Germany during the sixteenth century. This study partially supports Goehr's claim against critiques raised by various scholars *contra* the scarcity of her historical sources.

19 See also Glarean (1965).

20 For a further consideration of the argument regarding the *musica poetica*, see Strohm (2001).

21 For further reading, see Powers (1996).

22 See Dahlhaus (1977), Wiora (1983), and more recent analyses such as that by Strohm, entitled "'Opus': An Aspect of the Early History of the Musical Work-Concept," in Jex (2003: 309–319).

23 This vision of the historical evolution of the work- and author-concepts has been subsumed by Karol Berger in his theory of successive shifting paradigms, as articulated in the book *A Theory of Art* (Berger 2000: 133–134).

24 Whig historiography, influenced by Herbert Butterfield's 1931 book *The Whig Interpretation of History* (Butterfield 1965), is permeated by a sense of historical progress that conceives the past as a foreshadowing of an always greater and more enlightened present.

25 Let me mention, as a significant historical example, that music's progressive "disenchantment" linked the new roles that it came to play after the 1800s, when it assumed "a transcendental function that a declining religious practice could no longer provide" (Goehr 2007: 157).

26 For further reading, see Dorottya Fabian, "Towards a Performance History of Bach's Sonatas and Partitas for Solo Violin: Preliminary Investigations," in Vikárius and Lampert (2005: 87–108). The first renowned performers of Bach's Sonatas and Partitas were Franz Benda and his student Johann Peter Salomon, who became familiar with the music through C. P. E. Bach and performed it in London after 1781 (Unverricht 2017).

27 A significant scholarly contribution in this regard is John Kenneth Lutterman's dissertation (Lutterman 2006).

28 For a case in point, see Payne (1999). John Kenneth Lutterman points out, within a consideration of Bach's Suite for Solo Lute, that it is an example of the way in which the German composer seemed "to have entered into a dialogue with his own texts, using them in much the same way that he used the texts of other composers, giving them more elaborate figuration and appropriating ideas for other purposes, introducing new cultural voices, extending the discourse into new spheres" (Lutterman 2006: 41–42).

29 In Christoph Wolff's revised version of the *New Bach Reader*, which includes a comprehensive collection of Bach's letters and documents, the author points out that:

> Bach did not care to write about himself . . . [A]s far as we know, he never wrote a word concerning the aesthetic speculations or controversies of the time . . . [H]e was a practical musician and evidently had no desire to appear to be anything else. Yet he possessed a definite artistic creed.
>
> (Wolff *et al.* 1998: 16)

A narrowly selective list of historically relevant secondary sources that represents some of the dominant views at the time would include Printz (1696),

Kuhnau (1997), Niedt (2014), and Mattheson (2015). As I pointed out earlier in the consideration of Romantic authorship, a detailed consideration of musical authorship in Baroque treatises goes beyond the scope of the present book.

30 As examples consider Bach's arrangement of Johann Adam Reincken's *Hortus Musicus,* his fugues based on Tomaso Albionini's *Trio Sonatas* Op. 1, his redrafting of collections such as the *Art of the Fugue* or even the *Sei Solo a Violino*, his transcriptions of Italian concertos during the Weimar and Leipzig periods, and his adaption of works such as Giovanni Battista Pergolesi's *Stabat Mater*.

31 David Schulenberg explains, referring to J. S. Bach's scores, that "the surviving documents represent only the tip of the iceberg, the visible remains of musical practices and musical thought that are largely hidden to us, although perhaps not entirely unrecoverable" (Schulenberg 1995: 3–4).

32 Christopher Small uses the term "musicking" to highlight that music has a processual (verb) and objectual (noun) nature, he defines it on the following terms:

> To music is to take part, in any capacity, in a musical performance, whether by performing, by listening, by rehearsing or practicing, by providing material for performance (what is called composing), or by dancing. We might at times even extend its meaning to what the person is doing who takes the tickets at the door or the hefty men who shift the piano and the drums or the roadies who set up the instruments and carry out the sound checks or the cleaners who clean up after everyone else has gone. They, too, are all contributing to the nature of the event that is a musical performance.
>
> (Small 1998: 9)

33 Let me introduce here a small fragment written by Arthur Mendel and published on a collection of essays originally published in 1957:

> Western musicians of today have such strong habits of associating a piece of music with its graphic notation that they need constant reminding, by every possible means, of the limitations of notation as applied to either old or exotic music. The hunt for the authentic version of a piece by even so recent a composer as J.S. Bach (1685–1750), though one of the principal preoccupations of beginners in musicological interest, and the task that many "practical musicians" expect of musicologists, is a vain one. Neither Bach nor any other good musician up to at least Bach's time probably ever played a piece exactly the same way twice. And by "the same way" we mean nothing so narrow as the musician of today may understand. We mean that he probably never played exactly the same notes twice, or played them in exactly the same rhythm.
>
> (Mendel 1957: 10)

34 Lisa Giombini points out that "an ontological approach to musical works has dominated Anglo-Saxon aesthetics for almost fifty years" (Giombini 2015: 14).

35 As examples, see Cage (1973), Monelle (1992), Attali (2009), and Treitler (2011).

36 While analyzing the endless approaches to musical ontology that coexist in contemporary literature, Robert Stecker points out that "more recently the main debate seems to be about what type or kind a work of music is: an eternal structure, an indicated-type, a norm-kind" (Stecker 2009: 375).

37 The first one attempts to define the elements that determine the identity of a musical work, the second one attempts to explain to which ontological categories do musical works belong, and the last one attempts to regulate which examples or kinds of a given work (performances, scores, etc.) can be considered as legitimate or authentic representations of that work.
38 For example Andrew Kania's "New Waves in Musical Ontology" in Stock (2008: 20–40), Kivy (2002: 202–223), and Davies (2009: 744–755).
39 Figures 2.1 and 2.2 are a personal adaptation of the classificatory model introduced by Lisa Giombini (Giombini 2015: 19 and 107). While Table 2.2 refers only to the ontological discussions considered in this text, Figure 2.1 introduces a comprehensive summary that includes scholars not mentioned here, since the examination of their work and ideas would require addressing debates that go beyond my present purposes. Furthermore, we need to bear in mind that the divisions among the different approaches to musical ontology are not clear-cut: many writers have explored diverse perspectives or introduced readings that lay in the boundary-zones. As a matter of fact, this text looks at specific examples of the work of significant scholars that can be seen only as snippets of their developing discussions of musical ontology, snippets that are nonetheless necessary and sufficient to ground the overall argument that I am attempting to develop.
40 For a summary, see Davies (2011: 23–50), Giombini (2015), and Kania (2016).
41 See Goodman (1976, 1978) and Davies (2011: 59).
42 The inclusion of instrumental performance means in a discussion of the ontological status of musical works has been defined by David Davies as instrumentalism (Davies 2011: 33–34).
43 For a further discussion of Levinson's idea of contextualism, see Levinson (2006: 29).
44 Kivy points out that Platonism "captures a great many of our intuitions and musical *façons de parler*" (Kivy 1993: 35).
45 See also Dipert (1980: 206–207).
46 For an enlightening discussion of "universals," "types," "sets," and "kinds," see Wetzel (2014).
47 For further reading, see Davies (2001).
48 Numerical identity implies absolute sameness and can hold only between a thing and itself. Qualitative identity, on the other hand, takes place between things that share properties even if they are not numerically identical.
49 From a pure sonicist perspective, the instrumental and timbral dimensions of the work are not core identity–defining elements of their instantiations.
50 See also Dodd (2002, 2004). Dodd's ideas seem to echo some philosophic-mathematical commitments linked to elements found in the theoretical approaches of diverse mathematical realists, elements that he applies to the consideration of musical works and musical creativity. For further reading, see Resnik (2003).
51 An example of Dahlhaus's contribution to the what has become the umbrella term of systematic musicology, discussing some of the ideas explored here, can be found in Dahlhaus *et al.* (1982: 25–48).
52 For further reading, see Peter Lamarque (2002).
53 For a further discussion of Davies's adoption of Currie's multiple instance model, see Davies (2010: 411–426, 2004: 127–145).
54 Currie considered creativity as an act of discovery and was particularly interested on the heuristic path that unites the author and her/his work. For a further discussion of action-types, see Currie (1989: 46–84).

55 David Davies explains that antirealists, or what he terms fictionalists, giving the term a broader meaning than the one proposed here, claim that "while there are actually no such things as musical works, we have shared ways of representing such things in our musical practice . . . and this justifies continuing to talk as if there were such works even if the world contains no such things" (Davies 2011: 46).

56 The aesthetic paradigm is "committed to the view that aesthetics is to be considered as a completely independent discipline [from metaphysics], with its own purposes and *agenda* (sic)" (Giombini 2015: 137).

57 This notion is influenced by the Wittgensteinian ideas of unbounded concepts and family resemblances; for further reading, see Glock and Hyman (2017: 407–419).

58 In her book *Fiction and Metaphysics*, Thomasson seems happy to embrace a vision of the musical work that broadens Platonist readings by "allowing that we can have direct reference to and gain cognitive access to dependent abstracta by means of the space-time objects on which they depend" (Thomasson 1999: 54). Thomasson's position could be seen as a form of "qualified realism," but, given her meta-ontological critique of the traditional approaches, it is included here since it questions the methodological validity of the nature of the dominant ontological readings.

59 Compositional or mereological (related to the study of parts and wholes) nihilism is a philosophical position that argues that only mereological simples exist and that, as a result, nothing is a proper part of anything (Sider in Bennett and Zimmerman 2013: 237–239). For further reading, you may refer to the work of the analytic philosophers Peter Unger, Trento Merricks, and Peter van Inwagen.

60 Cameron defines himself as an ontological realist in an article entitled "How to Have a Radically Minimal Ontology." I argue that his meta-ontological critique might be seen as a form of "qualified realism" – as in Thomasson's case – but that, given its questioning of the traditional approaches, it can be included in the present antirealist section. See Ross Cameron (2010: 256). For further reading please refer to (Cameron 2015).

61 Following a similar line of thought, Kraut points out in *Artworld Metaphysics* that "considerable stretches of metaphysical dispute . . . are thus riddled with puzzles and communication breakdowns" (Kraut 2007: 152).

62 Goodman writes:

> Let us speak of a work of art as *autographic* if and only if the distinction between original and forgery of it is significant; or better, if and only if even the most exact duplication of it does not thereby count as genuine . . . Thus painting is autographic, music nonautographic, or *allographic*.
>
> (Goodman 1976: 113)

63 See also Cone (1968) and Derrida (1987: 15–148).

64 Essentialism in philosophy implies that "for a specific kind of entity, there is a set of properties that all entities of that kind must possess and by virtue of which it can be precisely defined or described" (Giombini 2015: 165). For further reading on essentialism and art, see Giombini (2015: 166–169).

65 Here Derrida is explicating Heidegger and introducing a processual and hence not-objectual vision of the work. The work is not the thing that emerges from an intentionally directed creative act but a process that reciprocally intertwines the

subject and its theme, the artistic gesture becoming one of "bearing" in lieu of one of "producing" (Derrida 1987).

66 A remarkable contribution in this regard has been made by Christy Mag Uidhir in Uidhir (2012: 1–26).

References

Agawu, Kofi. *Music as Discourse: Semiotic Adventures in Music Theory*. New York: Oxford University Press, 2009.

Almen, Byron. *A Theory of Musical Narrative*. Bloomington: Indiana University Press, 2008.

Alperson, Philip, ed. *What Is Music? An Introduction to the Philosophy of Music*. University Park: Pennsylvania State University Press, 1987.

Anscombe, Elisabeth. *Intention*. Cambridge, MA: Harvard University Press, 2000.

Arbo, Alessandro, and Marcello Ruta, eds. *Ontologie musicale: Perspectives et debats*. Paris: Hermann Editeurs, 2014.

Attali, Jacques. *Noise: The Political Economy of Music*. Minneapolis: University of Minnesota Press, 2009.

Barthes, Roland. *Mythologies*. New York: Hill & Wang, 1972.

———. *Image-Music-Text*. New York: Hill & Wang, 1977.

Bates, David. "Crisis between the Wars: Derrida and the Origins of Undecidability." *Representations* 90 (Spring 2005): 1–27.

Bennett, Andrew. *The Author*. New York: Routledge, 2005.

Bennett, Karen, and Dean W. Zimmerman, eds. *Oxford Studies in Metaphysics*, Vol. 8. New York: Oxford University Press, 2013.

Bent, Ian. *Music Theory in the Age of Romanticism*. Cambridge: Cambridge University Press, 1996.

Berger, Karol. *A Theory of Art*. New York: Oxford University Press, 2000.

Booth, Wayne. *The Rhetoric of Function*. Chicago: University of Chicago Press, 1961.

Bouveresse, Jacques. *Le mythe de l'interiorite*. Paris: Minuit, 1976.

Burke, Seán, ed. *Authorship: From Plato to the Postmodern: A Reader*. Edinburgh: Edinburgh University Press, 1995.

Butt, John, ed. *The Cambridge Companion to Bach*. Cambridge: Cambridge University Press, 1997.

Butt, John, and Tim Carter, eds. *The Cambridge History of Seventeenth-Century Music*. Cambridge: Cambridge University Press, 2005.

Butterfield, Herbert. *The Whig Interpretation of History*. New York: W. W. Norton & Company, 1965.

Cage, John. *Silence*. Middletown, CT: Wesleyan University Press, 1973.

Cameron, Ross P. "There Are No Things That Are Musical Works." *British Journal of Aesthetics* 48, no. 3 (July 2008): 295–314.

———. "How to Have a Radically Minimal Ontology." *Philosophical Studies: An International Journal for Philosophy in the Analytic Tradition* 151, no. 2 (November 2010): 249–264.

———. *The Moving Spotlight: An Essay on Time and Ontology*. New York: Oxford University Press, 2015.

Clifford, James, and George E. Marcus, eds. *Writing Culture: The Poetics and Politics of Ethnography*. Berkeley: University of California Press, 1986.

Cobussen, Marcel. "Deconstruction in Music." PhD diss., Erasmus University Rotterdam, 2002.

Compagno, Dario. "Theories of Authorship and Intention in the Twentieth Century: An Overview." *Journal of Early Modern Studies* 1, no. 1 (2012): 37–53.

Cone, Edward T. *Musical Form and Musical Performance*. New York: W. W. Norton & Company, 1968.

Croce, Benedetto. *The Aesthetic as the Science of Expression and of the Linguistic in General*. Cambridge: Cambridge University Press, 1992.

Currie, Gregory. *An Ontology of Art*. New York: Palgrave Macmillan, 1989.

Dahlhaus, Carl. *Grundlagen der Musikgeshichte*. Cologne: Musikverlag Hans Gerig, 1977.

Dahlhaus, Carl, and H. de la Motte-Haber, eds. *Systematische Musikwissenschaft*. Wiesbaden, Germany: Akademische Verlagsgesellschaft Athenaion, 1982, available from https://www.amazon.de/SYSTEMATISCHE-MUSIKWISSENSCHAFT-Carl-Dahlhaus/dp/3799707522.

———. *The Idea of Absolute Music*. Chicago: University of Chicago Press, 1989.

Dahlhaus, Carl, Ruth E. Muller, and Friederick Zaminer. *Die Musiktheorie im 18. Und 19. Jahrhundert; Geschichte der Musiktheorie, Bd. 11*. Darmstadt: Wissenschaftliche Buchegesellschaft, 1984.

Davies, David. "Artistic Intentions and the Ontology of Art." *British Journal of Aesthetics* 39, no. 2 (April 1999): 148–162.

———. *Art as Performance*. Oxford: Blackwell, 2004.

———. "The Primacy of Practice in the Ontology of Art." *The Journal of Aesthetics and Art Criticism* 67, no. 2 (Spring 2009): 159–171.

———. *Philosophy of the Performing Arts*. Oxford: Wiley-Blackwell, 2011.

Davies, Stephen. "The Aesthetic Relevance of Authors' and Painters' Intentions." *The Journal of Aesthetics and Art-Criticism* 41, no. 1 (Autumn 1982): 65–76.

———. "Platonism in Music: Another Kind of Defense." *American Philosophical Quarterly* 24, no. 3 (July 1987): 245–252.

———. "Reviewed Work(s): The Work of Music and the Problem of its Identity by Roman Ingarden, Adam Czerniawski and Jean G. Harrell." *Journal of Music Theory* 32, no. 1 (Spring 1988): 169–176.

———. "The Ontology of Musical Works and the Authenticity of Their Performances." *Noûs* 25, no. 1 (March 1991): 21–41.

———. *Musical Works and Performances: A Philosophical Exploration*. New York: Oxford University Press, 2001.

———. *Themes in the Philosophy of Music*. New York: Oxford University Press, 2003.

———. "Musical Works and Orchestral Color." *British Journal of Aesthetics* 48, no. 4 (2008): 363–375.

Deleuze, Gilles, and Félix Guattari. *What Is Philosophy?* New York: Columbia University Press, 1994.

Derrida, Jacques. *Of Grammatology*. Baltimore: Johns Hopkins University Press, 1976.
———. *Signéponge/Signsponge*. New York: Columbia University Press, 1984.
———. *The Truth in Painting*. Chicago: University of Chicago Press, 1987.
———. *The Work of Mourning*. Chicago: University of Chicago Press, 2001.
Dipert, Randall R. "The Composer's Intentions: An Examination of Their Relevance for Performance." *Musical Quarterly* 66 (1980): 205–218.
Dodd, Julian. "Musical Works as Eternal Types." *British Journal of Aesthetics* 40 (2000): 420–440.
———. "Defending Musical Platonism." *The British Journal of Aesthetics* 42, no. 4 (October 2002): 380–402.
———. "Types, Continuants, and the Ontology of Music." *The British Journal of Aesthetics* 44, no. 4 (October 2004): 342–360.
———. *Works of Music: An Essay in Ontology*. New York: Oxford University Press, 2007.
Eagleton, Terry. *Literary Theory: An Introduction*. Minneapolis: University of Minnesota Press, 1983.
Eco, Umberto. *A Theory of Semiotics*. Bloomington: Indiana University Press, 1979.
———. *The Open Work*. Cambridge, MA: Cambridge University Press, 1989.
Erauw, Willem. "Canon Formation: Some More Reflections on Lydia Goehr's Imaginary Museum of Musical Works." *Acta Musicologica* 71 (1998): 109–115.
Forkel, Johann Nikolaus. *Über Johann Sebastian Bachs Leben, Kunst und Kunstwerke*, ed. Joseph Müller-Blattau. Kassel und Basle: Bärenreiter-Verlag, 1950.
Foucault, Michel. *The Foucault Reader*. New York: Pantheon, 1984.
Gallope, Michael. "Is There a Deleuzian Musical Work?" *Perspectives of New Music* 46, no. 2 (Summer 2008): 93–129.
Giombini, Lisa. "Music, Restoration, Performance and Ontology: A Guide for the Perplexed." PhD diss., Universita degli Studi 'Roma Tre' and Université de Lorraine, 2015.
Glarean, Henricus. *Dodecachordon*. Mergelberg: American Institute of Musicology, 1965.
Glock, Hans-Johann, and John Hyman, eds. *A Companion to Wittgenstein*. Oxford: Wiley Blackwell, 2017.
Goehr, Lydia. *The Imaginary Museum of Musical Works: An Essay in the Philosophy of Music*. New York: Oxford University Press, 2007.
Goodman, Nelson. *Languages of Art*. Indianapolis, IN: Hackett Publishing Company, 1976.
———. *Ways of Worldmaking*. Indianapolis, IN: Hackett Publishing Company, 1978.
Greenblatt, Stephen. *Learning to Curse: Essays in Early Modern Culture*. New York: Routledge, 1990.
Hegel, George W. F. *Aesthetics: Lectures on Fine Art*, Vol. 2. Oxford: Clarendon Press, 1975.
Hoffmann, Ernst T. A. *E. T. A. Hoffmann's Musical Writings: Kreisleriana: The Poet and the Composer; Music Criticism*. Cambridge: Cambridge University Press, 1989.

Hunter, Mary. "'To Play as If from the Soul of the Composer': The Idea of the Performer in Early Romantic Aesthetics." *Journal of the American Musicological Society* 58, no. 2 (Summer 2005): 357–398.

Husserl, Edmund. *Logical Investigations*, Vol. 1. New York: Routledge, 1970.

Ingarden, Roman. "Artistic and Aesthetics Values." *British Journal of Aesthetics* 4, no. 3 (1964): 198–213.

———. *The Work of Music and the Problem of Its Identity*. Berkeley: University of California Press, 1986.

———. *Ontology of the Work of Art: The Musical Work, the Picture, the Architectural Work, the Film*. Athens: Ohio University Press, 1989.

Jacobus, Mary. *Reading Woman: Essays in Feminist Criticism*. London: Methuen, 1986.

Jex, Tomasz, ed. *Complexus Effectuum Musicologiae: Studia Miroslao Perz Septuagenario Deidicata*. Krakow: Studia et Dissertationes Instituti Musicologiae Universitatis Varsoviensis, 2003.

Kania, Andrew. "Piece for the End of Time: In Defence of Musical Ontology." *British Journal of Aesthetics* 48, no. 1 (January 2008): 65–79.

———. "The Philosophy of Music." *The Stanford Encyclopedia of Philosophy* (Winter 2016 Edition), Edward N. Zalta (ed.), available from https://plato.stanford.edu/archives/win2016/entries/music

Kivy, Peter. "Platonism in Music: Another Kind of Defense." *American Philosophical Quarterly* 24, no. 3 (July 1987): 245–252.

———. *The Fine Art of Repetition*. New York: Cambridge University Press, 1993.

———. *Authenticities: Philosophical Reflections on Musical Performance*. Ithaca: Cornell Publishing, 1995.

———. *Introduction to a Philosophy of Music*. New York: Oxford University Press, 2002.

Krausz, Michael, Denis Dutton, and Karen Beardsley, eds. *The Idea of Creativity*. Boston: Brill, 2009.

Kraut, Robert. *Artworld Metaphysics*. New York: Oxford University Press, 2007.

———. "Universals, Metaphysical Explanations, and Pragmatism." *The Journal of Philosophy* 107, no. 11 (November 2010): 590–609.

———. "Ontology: Music and Art." *The Monist* 95, no. 4 (October 2012): 684–710.

Kuhnau, Johann. *The Musical Charlatan*. New York: Camden House, 1997.

Lamarque, Peter. "Work and Object." *Proceedings of the Aristotelian Society: New Series* 102 (2002): 41–162.

———. *Work and Object: Explorations in the Metaphysics of Art*. New York: Oxford University Press, 2012.

Leader, Zachary. *Revision and Romantic Authorship*. New York: Oxford University Press, 2000.

Levinson, Jerrold. "What a Musical Work Is." *The Journal of Philosophy* 77, no. 1 (January 1980): 5–28.

———. *Contemplating Art: Essays in Aesthetics*. New York: Oxford University Press, 2006.

———. "Aesthetic Contextualism." *Postgraduate Journal of Aesthetics* 4, no. 3 (2007).
———. *Music, Art and Metaphysics*. New York: Oxford University Press, 2011.
Levi-Strauss, Claude. *The Raw and the Cooked*. Chicago: University of Chicago Press, 1969.
Listenius, Nikolai. *Music: Ad authore denuo recognita multisque novis regulis et exemplis adaucta*. Berlin: G. Schuneman, 1927.
Liszt, Franz. *Selected Letters*. New York: Oxford University Press, 1999.
Littlefield, Richard C. "The Silence of the Frames." *Music Theory Online* 2, no. 1 (January 1996), available from www.mtosmt.org/issues/mto.96.2.1/mto.96.2.1.littlefield.html
Loesch, Heinz von. *Der Werkbegriff in Der Protestantischen Musiktheorie Des 16. Und 17. Jahrhunderts: Ein Missverständnis, Studien Zur Geschichte Der Musiktheorie*. New York: Olms, 2001.
Lutterman, John Kenneth. "Works in Progress: J. S. Bach's Suites for Solo Cello as Artifacts of Improvisatory Practices." PhD diss., University of California, 2006.
Marx, Adolf B. *The Music of the Nineteenth Century and Its Culture*. Cambridge: Cambridge University Press, 2009.
Mattheson, Johann. *Der vollkommene Capellmeister*. Emeryville, CA: Andesite Press, 2015.
Mendel, Arthur, ed. *Some Aspects of Musicology*. New York: Liberal Arts Press, 1957.
Merrell, Floyd. *Semiosis in the Postmodern Age*. West Lafayette, IN: Purdue University Press, 1995.
Moi, Toril. *Sexual/Textual Politics: Feminist Literary Theory*. London: Methuen, 1985.
Monelle, Raymond. *Linguistics and Semiotics in Music*. New York: Routledge, 1992.
Nattiez, Jean-Jacques. *Music and Discourse: Towards a Semiology of Music*. Princeton, NJ: Princeton University Press, 1990.
Neubauer, John, *et al*. *New Paths: Aspects of Music Theory and Aesthetics in the Age of Romanticism*. Leuven: Leuven University Press, 2009.
Niedt, Friedrich Erhard. *Musicalische Handleitung, oder Gründlicher Unterricht*. Charleston, NC: Nabu Press, 2014.
Osmond-Smith, David. "Formal Iconism in Music." *Versus: Quaderni di Studi Semiotici* 5 (1973): 43–54.
Palazzetti, Nicolo. "Reviewed Work(s): Ontologie musicale – Perspectives et debats." *International Review of the Aesthetics and Sociology of Music* 46, no. 1 (June 2015): 190–193.
Palfy, Cora Suzanne. "Musical Agency as an Intersubjective Phenomenon." PhD diss., Northwestern University, 2015.
Pareyson, Luigi. *Existence, Interpretation, Freedom: Selected Readings*. Aurora, CO: Davies Group Publishers, 2009.

Payne, Ian. "Telemann's Musical Style c. 1709–c. 1730 and J. S. Bach: The Evidence of Borrowing." *Bach* 30, no. 1 (Spring–Summer 1999): 42–64.

Perkins, Leeman P. "Concerning the Ontological Status of the Notated Musical Work in the Fifteenth and Sixteenth Centuries." *Current Musicology* 75 (Spring 2002): 15–39.

Pousseur, Henri. *Musique, Semantique, Societe*. Paris: Casterman, 1972.

Powers, Harold. "A Canonical Museum of Imaginary Music." *Current Musicology* 60/61 (Spring/Fall 1996): 5–25.

Printz, Wolfgang C. *Phrynis Mitilenaeus, oder Satyrischer Componist*. Leipzig: Johann Christoph Mieth & Johann Christoph Zimmermann, 1696, available from http://reader.digitale-sammlungen.de/de/fs1/object/display/bsb11173631_00003.html

Resnik, Michale D. "What Is Mathematical Realism?" *Oxford Scholarship Online* (November 2003), available from www.oxfordscholarship.com/view/10.1093/0198250142.001.0001/acprof-9780198250142-chapter-2

Ridley, Aaron. "Against Musical Ontology." *The Journal of Philosophy* 100, no. 4 (April 2003): 203–220.

———. *The Philosophy of Music: Theme and Variations*. Edinburgh: Edinburgh University Press, 2004.

Rohrbaugh, Guy. "Artworks as Historical Individuals." *European Journal of Philosophy* 11, no. 2 (2003): 177–205.

———. "I Could Have Done That." *British Journal of Aesthetics* 45, no. 3 (July 2005): 209–228.

Rudner, Richard. "The Ontological Status of the Esthetic Object." *Philosophy and Phenomenological Research* 10, no. 3 (March 1950): 380–388.

Ruta, Marcello. "Is There an Ontological Musical Common Sense?" *Aisthesis. Pratiche, linguaggi e saperi dell'estetico* 6, no. 3 (February 2014), available from www.fupress.net/index.php/aisthesis/article/view/14096/13086

Ruwet, Nicolas. *Language, Musique, Poesie*. Paris: Seuil, 1972.

Schelling, Friedrich W. J. *The Philosophy of Art*. Minneapolis: University of Minnesota Press, 1989.

Schulenberg, David. "Composition and Improvisation in the School of J. S. Bach." *Bach Perspectives* 1 (1995): 1–42.

Schumann, Robert. *Schumann on Music: A Selection from the Writings*. New York: Dover Publications, 1988.

Scruton, Roger. *The Aesthetics of Music*. New York: Oxford University Press, 1997.

Sheinberg, Esti. *Music Semiotics: A Network of Significations: In Honour and Memory of Raymond Monelle*. Burlington: Ashgate, 2012.

Showalter, Elaine, ed. *The New Feminist Criticism: Essays on Women, Literature, and Theory*. London: Virago, 1986.

Small, Christopher. *Musicking: The Meanings of Performing and Listening*. Middletown, CT: Wesleyan University Press, 1998.

Stecker, Robert. "Methodological Questions about the Ontology of Music." *The Journal of Aesthetics and Art Criticism* 67, no. 4 (Fall 2009): 375–386.

Stefani, Gino. "Semiotique en musicology." *Versus: Quaderni di Studi Semiotici* 5 (1973): 20–42.

Steiner, Wendi. *The Sign in Music and Literature*. Austin: University of Texas Press, 1981.

Stock, Kathleen, and Katherine Thomson-Jones, eds. *New Waves in Aesthetics*. London: Palgrave Macmillan, 2008.

Strohm, Reinhard. *Music as Concept and Practice in the Late Middle Ages*. Oxford: Oxford University Press, 2001.

Talbot, Michael, ed. *The Musical Work: Reality or Invention*. Liverpool: Liverpool University Press, 2000.

Tarasti, Ero. *A Theory of Musical Semiotics*. Bloomington: Indiana University Press, 1994.

Thomasson, Amie L. *Fiction and Metaphysics*. New York: Cambridge University Press, 1999.

———. "The Ontology of Art and Knowledge in Aesthetics." *The Journal of Aesthetics and Art Criticism* 63, no. 3 (Summer 2005): 221–229.

Tillman, Chris. "Musical Materialism." *British Journal of Aesthetics* 51, no. 1 (January 2011): 13–29.

Treitler, Leo. *Reflections on Musical Meaning and Its Representations*. Bloomington: Indiana University Press, 2011.

Uidhir, Christy Mag, ed. *Art & Abstract Objects*. New York: Oxford University Press, 2012.

Unverricht, Hubert. "Salomon, Johann Peter." *Grove Music Online: Oxford Music Online*. Oxford University Press, 2017.

Vikárius, László, and Vera Lampert, eds. *Essays in Honor of László Somfai: Studies in the Sources and Interpretation of Music*. Lanham, MD: Scarecrow Press, 2005.

Waugh, Patricia. *Literary Theory and Criticism: An Oxford Guide*. Oxford: Oxford University Press, 2006.

Wetzel, Linda. "Types and Tokens." *The Stanford Encyclopedia of Philosophy* (Spring 2014 Edition), Edward N. Zalta (ed.), available from https://plato.stanford.edu/archives/spr2014/entries/types-tokens

Wimsatt, William Kurtz, and Monroe Beardsley. *The Verbal Icon: Studies in the Meaning of Poetry*. Lexington: Kentucky University Press, 1954.

Wiora, Walter. *Das Musikalisch Kunstwerk*. Tutzing: Hans Schneider, 1983.

Wittgenstein, Ludwig. *Major Works: Selected Philosophical Writings*. New York: Harper Perennial Modern Classics, 2009.

Wolff, Christoph, Hans T. David, and Arthur Mendel, eds. *The Bach Reader: A Life of Johann Sebastian Bach in Letters and Documents*. London: W. W. Norton & Company, 1998.

Wolterstoff, Nicholas. *Works and Worlds of Art*. New York: Oxford University Press, 1980.

3 Barthes and Derrida

Terminology and methodology

Post-structuralist thinking has been a continual source of academic inspiration since the 1960s. After an initial boom of related scholarly work that influenced not only literary criticism and philosophy but most humanistic disciplines, post-structuralist theories receded into a lower level of academic ubiquity, especially in the United States, as new approaches became prevalent in the late 1980s.[1] Post-structuralist ideas have nonetheless remained significant as referential models for emergent critical theories.

The variety of approaches found in previous adaptations of post-structural elements into musical discourses makes necessary an introductory clarification of the intellectual standpoint articulated in this book.[2] My reading avoids a direct transposition of analytical or theoretical frameworks, deemed as an overt imposition of alien concept-structures. I do not attempt to mirror Derridean deconstruction.[3] Instead, I explore how specific elements of Barthes's and Derrida's intellectual worlds can be adapted into a discussion of music-related issues. I argue that those recurring ideas or "intellectual gestures" that Marian Hobson defines as the "strange attractors" found in the "circuits of argument" that characterize the French thinker's thematized writings might be used to this end.[4] Furthermore, I believe that only a few intellectuals have managed to bridge, at least partially, the chasm emerging during the past and current centuries between the development of new critical theories in the humanities and their application to music scholarship.[5] I acknowledge my role as an outsider, as a performer and musicologist fascinated by the intellectual potential of some post-structuralist notions and working critical frameworks. The reconsideration of musical authorship and of the work-concept introduced here and the analytical approaches explored in the final part of the text, which are highly indebted to some of those intellectual gestures – openly levitating around those "strange attractors" – legitimize the nature of such a personal standpoint. Despite Barthes's and especially Derrida's view of their own work as nonmethodological and the fact that the malleable, unstable, even polyhedral meanings of their (non) concepts usually lay outside the boundaries of the definable, I will briefly consider them here – subjecting them to a semantic analysis – in order to expose their implications, facilitate their use, and justify their central role in the remainder of the text. As a matter of fact, the conception of the . . . *Bach* . . . project would not have been possible without the example provided by the French thinkers' nonmethodological approach: as I pointed out earlier, the . . . *Bach* . . . project parallels their attempt to embrace, embody, expand, and deconstruct the notion of the work beyond its potential judicability, beyond its conditions of truth and falsity.

Barthes and the "Death of the Author"

Two short articles, "The Death of the Author" and "From Work to Text" (originally published in 1968 and 1971 and both included in the 1977 book *Image-Music-Text*), will bear a greater impact on the music-analytical perspective introduced in Chapter 4.[6] The former article will be examined here as it conveys some key elements of Barthes's understanding of authorship. The latter will be revisited on the final reflections introduced in the book's concluding lines.

As we have seen, Barthes's "The Death of the Author" was a key contribution to the postmodern reshaping of the notion of authorship. Barthes favored readings of the text that opposed the former focus on objective analysis and explored instead anarchical approaches, based in linguistics, psychoanalysis, and anthropology. Since Barthes viewed the author's intention as an undue constraint on the reader's freedom, he proposed that, given the inaccessibility of an original master meaning or intention, "the birth of the reader must be at the cost of the death of the Author" (Barthes 1977: 148). This idea provides a powerful framework to understand the questioning of the dominant notion of authorship posited by the . . . *Bach* . . . project. It is in this light that music, as literature, can be understood as the quagmire where all identity, including that of the body that writes, is lost.

Following the previous argument, Barthes defined the figure of the author as a modern notion, "a product of our society insofar as, emerging from at the end of the Middle Ages with English empiricism, French rationalism and the personal faith of the Reformation, it discovered the prestige of the individual" (Ibid.: 142–143). Consequently, the modern author-concept, as that of the closed work, cannot be conceived as a given but as a historically determined and evolving regulative idea, one that parallels Goehr's "historicist" reading. This historical shaping has led to an image of literature in contemporary culture that "is tyrannically centered on the author, his person, his history, his tastes, his passions" (Ibid.: 143). From Barthes's perspective, the text cannot be seen as a "line of words, releasing a single 'theological' meaning (the 'message' of the Author-God) but a multidimensional space in which a variety of writings, none of them original, blend and clash. The text is a tissue of citations, resulting from the innumerable centers [*sources*] of culture" (Ibid.: 146). The writer thus imitates a gesture forever anterior, never original. The negation of the traditional author-role makes the need to decipher the text unnecessary, even absurd, since:

> [i]n the multiplicity of writing, everything is to be *disentangled*, but nothing *deciphered*; the structure can be followed, "run" [*threaded*] . . . at every point and at every level, but there is nothing beneath [*no underlying ground*]: the space of the writing is to be ranged over [*traversed*], not pierced; writing ceaselessly posits meaning ceaselessly to evaporate it, carrying out a systematic exemption of meaning.
>
> (Ibid.: 147; italics mine)

This new vision of the text consists, as in the . . . *Bach* . . . project, of multiple writings "drawn from many cultures and entering into mutual relations of dialogue, parody, contestation" (Ibid.: 148). The text thus becomes an "infinite text," and the reader becomes the *locus* where this textual multiplicity is pulled together: the unity of the text has been displaced from its origin to its destination, from its *terminus a quo* to its *terminus ad quem*.

The fact that Barthes's "Death of the Author" was written in 1967 and first published in 1968, the year of *les événements*, made it acquire a unique historical iconicity.[7] Given the revolutionary style and the condensed nature of the text, it seemingly adopted the form of a literary manifesto that became, eventually, a slogan.[8] As such, the "Death of Author" has been endlessly (re)examined and subjected to thorough critical scrutiny. A common germane critique points out that Barthes's "romantic author" was a nonstanding referent by 1967: it had already been questioned and partially dismantled by the Russian Formalists and Anglo-American New Criticism. Seán Burke stresses that:

> Barthes himself, in seeking to dethrone the author, is led to an apotheosis of authorship that vastly outplaces anything to be found in the critical history he takes arms against . . . Barthes's entire polemic is grounded in the false assumption that if a magisterial status is denied . . . then the very concept of the author itself becomes otiose.
>
> (Burke 1992: 27)

Burke argues that Barthes's author became a metaphysical abstraction, a Platonic type, a fiction of the absolute that haunted his subsequent writings. This explains why, in his following books, Barthes attempted to articulate a return of the author instituted by the reader's desire for a restoration that would not challenge the author's pre-assumed demise: "a little like Dionysus, or Christ, the author must be dead before he can return. In a sense too, he must continue to be dead though he has returned" (Burke 1992: 30). A return is defined as "friendly" by Barthes in *Sade, Fourier, Loyola* (1971), when he writes that "the pleasure of the Text includes . . . the amicable return of the author," and mentioned again in *The Pleasure of the Text* (1974), when he points out that "as an institution, the author is dead: his person . . . has disappeared . . . but in the text, in a certain way, I *desire* the author" (Barthes 1989: 8, 1975: 27). A further analysis of Barthes's subsequent considerations of authorship is not central to the discussion raised in this text and goes beyond the scope of the argument that I am trying to develop. The inclusion of Barthes's "Death of the Author" here is not naïve or cursory, though: the article presents some critical intellectual gestures that can be connected to the ensuing examination of Derridean terminology and that will prove to have a greater bearing when applied to the still dominantly Romantic author- and work-concepts that permeate twentieth-century and contemporary musicology. Let us now turn to a consideration of Derrida's work and ideas.

Derridean terminology

The key notions explored in this book, defined by Hobson as *lexemes*, reoccur throughout Derrida's output (Hobson 1998: 3). However, I have chosen to focus here on a limited selection of early seminal texts, such as *Of Grammatology* (1967), *Writing and Difference* (1967), *Dissemination* (1972), *Margins of Philosophy* (1982), and *Limited Inc* (1988). The following section introduces brief reflections on the meaning(s) of these key ideas and their potential application(s) to music. The reader should not assume, though, that this terminological selection is intended to be comprehensive or to represent the plurality and complexity of Derrida's thinking. I have considered instead the terms that will have a bearing on the following analytical section, which examines case studies from the . . . *Bach* . . . project. Furthermore, these idioms have to be understood as flexible patterns of organization or circuits of argument rather than closed or stable units of meaning. They reappear and evolve throughout Derrida's writings, they "cannot be put into an array, they do not seem to have a common form, *eidos*, nor concept. Each may be seen as the head of a filiatory line, by which they replicate, they engender doubles" (Hobson 1998: 67). Derrida himself referred to these *lexemes* as quasi-transcendentals. In *Limited Inc*, dealing with the idea of "iterability," he argued that this *lexeme*, like the others:

> Might belong *without* belonging to the class of concepts of which it must render an accounting, to the theoretical space that it organizes in

> a (as I often say) "quasi"-transcendental manner, is doubtless a proposition that might seem paradoxical, even contradictory in the eyes of common sense or of a rigid classic logic. It is perhaps unthinkable in the logic of such good sense.
>
> (Derrida 1997: 127)

Dissémination

Derrida expanded Barthes's polysemic model as developed in *S/Z*[9] to include the prospects of the literary emergence and suspension of meaning and to make possible the understanding of a text as an event rather than as a static formal convention.[10] Derrida adopted the term *dissémination*, borrowed from Stéphane Mallarmé, to refer to this "excess of meaning that was always both *more than* and *otherwise than* the plurality of meaning" (Hill 2007: 54). *Dissémination* thus replaces the hermeneutic concept of polysemy,

> The quasi-"meaning" of dissemination is the impossible return to the rejoined, readjusted unity of meaning, and the impeded march of any such *reflection*. But is dissemination then the *loss* of that kind of truth, the *negative* prohibition of all access to such a signified? Far from presupposing that a virgin substance thus precedes or oversees it, dispersing or withholding in a negative second moment, dissemination *affirms* the always already divided generation of meaning. Dissemination – spills it in advance.
>
> (Derrida 1981a: 268)

Textuality, understood as dissemination and dispersal of meaning, as intertextual weaving, becomes an unstoppable dynamic process. From this perspective, the . . . *Bach* . . . project can be seen as a web of recontextualizations, one that carries meanings and reveals connections that "were not only unintended on the composer's part, but that he could not even have imagined" (Cobussen 2002: 51), dissemination becoming (in a way) a compositional principle. Derrida argues that each quoted text continues to "radiate back toward the site of its removal, transforming that, too, as it affects the new territory. Each is defined (thought) by the operation and is at the same time defining (thinking) as far as the rules and effects of the operation are concerned" (Derrida 1981a: 355). In the . . . *Bach* . . . project, this double gesture affects both the original and the newly developing textuality, a symbiotic saprophytic relation of parasitism emerging between them.[11]

Furthermore, if each sign refers to something other than itself, meaning becomes inexhaustible, and its dispersion necessarily escapes the author's "original" intention. Following Barthes, Derrida points out that, once a text is made public, it gains an autonomy that shatters the author/work coincidence, with only authorial traces remaining as markers of the creative action. Textuality is thus characterized by its multiplicity: the multiplicity of readings in . . . *Bach* . . . attempts to demonstrate this:

> Instead of searching for unity, attention is shifted to the plurality of the text; there is no question of attempting to present any kind of unity. Each reading is partial by definition. It is an investigation of a part of the inexhaustible possibilities of each text (*texte pluriel*).
>
> (Cobussen 2002: 213)

Signature and iterability

The question of *signature(s)* is one of the key overarching concerns that unifies Derrida's output. One of his most notorious texts on the matter, entitled "Signature Event Context," was originally published in 1971 and included a critical discussion of some of the ideas introduced by the British philosopher of language John Langshaw Austin in his book, *How to Do Things with Words* (Derrida 1986: 307–330). Austin considered "signatures" to be written performative utterances, that is, non-truth-evaluable assertions that imply the doing of some kind of action.[12] A signature, to put it differently, attests a presence to "consciousness of a signifying intention at a particular moment" (Culler 1982: 125), while being a special "event whereby the unique signs itself doubly – you need to counter-sign at least once for a signature to be valid – and thus ends its uniqueness" (Hobson 1998: 111). Following this line of argument, Derrida pointed out that the "condition of possibility" of the effects associated with signing and signature (the fact that each signature is singular and unique) is, at the same time, the "condition of their impossibility" (the fact that each signature must be repeatable), what he termed as the "*double blind* of a signature event" (Derrida 1984: 64):

> In order to function, that is, to be readable, a signature must have a repeatable, iterable, imitable form; it must be detached from the present and singular intention of its production. It is its sameness, which, by corrupting its identity and its singularity, divides its seal.
>
> (Derrida 1986: 328–329)[13]

As a result, the notion of "iterability" (or repeatability), a term derived from the Greek *iter* (again) and linked to that of imitation, becomes central to understanding the Derridean vision of *signature*, even if it has much broader implications. Derrida argues that any discourse or signifying sequence needs to be iterable: "imitation is not an accident that befalls an original but its condition of possibility" (Culler 1982: 120). Put differently, all discourse is marked by its repeatability in that "however deeply embedded in the context or processes of its circumstances of production, it is repeatable in other circumstances applicable elsewhere" (Hobson 1998: 97). Derrida introduces a further duplication of the meaning of "iterability" by tracing the philological relation between the terms "iter" and "alter," claiming that to be repeatable is to be alterable. Iterability thus renders the stability of essence impossible since even an identical repetition implies an alteration, the emergence of difference/*différance*, through a two-part structural relation.

Derrida outlined three main "modalities of the signature," which was conceived either as an authenticating act, as "idiomatic" style, or as a reflexive short-circuit.[14] Following the second reading, a "style" can be understood as a collection of characteristic features that, once isolated, can be repeated and therefore altered. It is there that iterability becomes manifest "in the inauthentic, the derivative, the imitative, the parodic" elements that, by negating it, make possible the original and the authentic (Culler 1982: 120). As Derrida points out, "iterability makes possible idealization – and thus, a certain identity in repetition that is independent of the multiplicity of factual events – while at the same time limiting the idealization it makes possible: *broaching* and *breaching* it at once" (Derrida 1997: 61). The Dutch scholar Marcel Cobussen applies these notions to music when he argues:

> Iterability is always inscribed, and therefore necessarily inscribed, as a possibility in the functional structure of the musical mark, be it a note or a fragment, a whole composition or a complete body of works. Iterability entails both the "faithful" or conventional repetition of a piece of music, as well as its transgression or transformation. All music can, in principle, be repeated; thus, it automatically brings its own altering with it, dividing and displacing in accordance with the logical force of the "iter."
>
> (Cobussen 2002: 46)

Furthermore, Cobussen stresses that the presence of the composer's signature, as a sign of completion and closure, conceals the complex production process that precedes the idealized *opus perfectum*. The centrality of the composer's intention can thus be questioned, following Derrida's reading of Emmanuel Lévinas's view of his own work as a linear nonreturning path from the same (understood as the author's subjectivity or ego) to the other (the alterity or otherness represented by everything outside that authorial-self), a work possessed by a *dehiscence* (Ibid.: 188). A similar questioning takes place in the . . . *Bach* . . . project: the expansion or re-elaboration of

Bach's music seems to return the text back to its author, by placing a mirror that, through an inversion of the unidirectional same/other linkage, returns a letter to its dead remitter. This epistolary exchange attempts to revive the German composer from his Barthesian death, hence paradoxically reflecting on what Derrida and Lévinas defined as a nonreflective gesture – a linear nonreturning path. As Cobussen points out, analyzing Gerd Zacher's project *Die Kunst einer Fugue*, "the contribution of the other composers constitutes a surfeit of un-heard alterity" (Ibid.: 189). The . . . *Bach* . . . project aims to dilute the boundaries between composition, performance, and musicology. It also dislocates and thus problematizes the relationship between the authors and their texts:

> The border between interpretation (citation) and autonomous composition shifts. The "original" text remains intact; Bach remains present . . . The individuality of the other composers sounds strange in this work, as though it originates from another context . . . Bach's individuality sounds strange in this work, as though it originates from another context. Presence dissolves in absence. Presence dissolves in presence.
>
> (Ibid.: 192)

Archi-écriture

Derrida attempted to question the "logo-" and "phonocentrism" that had historically dominated the metaphysical opposition of speech and writing, underpinned by a distinction between the intelligible and the sensible derived from classical Greek philosophy, by introducing the idea of *archi-écriture* or "arche-writing."[15] "Phonocentrism" does not imply an innocent and equipolar opposition but a "hierarchy, where traditionally speech is held to be both superior to and more fundamental than writing" (Hobson 1998: 12). Against this dominant underlying ideal, the French author conceives speech as a form, or vocal subspecie, of "writing" or "writing-in-general." Therefore, "writing" becomes an "*archi-écriture*, an archi-writing or proto-writing which is the condition of both speech and writing in the narrow sense" and which renders their relationship supplemental (Culler 1982: 102). Arche-writing can be further stretched, beyond the written and spoken word to refer to anything "that gives rise to an inscription in general, whether it is literal or not, and even if what it distributes in space is alien to the order of the voice: cinematography, choreography, of course, but also pictorial, musical, sculptural 'writing'" (Derrida 1976: 9). Arche-writing thus expands the conception of the text to include what Derrida defines as all possible referents, context becoming an inner textual element instead of an extrinsic otherness. Cobussen takes these ideas as a point of departure to develop a powerful argument, regarding the understanding of music as text at three, interrelated plateaus:

> First, the discursive institutions, constitutive orders of knowledge and power that identify music as art, as culture, and as a "social field" are textual. Second, the representation of music, of listening to music, in language is (of course) textual. And third, music as sound, music as a spatial, temporal, and sense event, is a text. I consider the activity of performance, the experience of audition, and sound itself texts to the same extent as the notational text of the score. Furthermore, a musical text involves the possibility of other versions with similar structures (for example, any performance or interpretation), intertextual elements from other (musical) texts that are co-present with the musical text, and a general musical language in which the musical text participates.
>
> (Cobussen 2002: 21)

The questioning of authorship articulated by the . . . *Bach* . . . project dwells on this vision. The relationship between those textual dimensions has historically shifted to place the written text, the score – epitomizing the crystalized objectual dimension of the work – as the center and reference of most musical endeavors, especially within classical music scholarship, through a process that Lydia Goehr has defined as a form of "conceptual imperialism." This book aims to reconsider and rearticulate the relationship between music's multiple textualities in order to posit a renewed conception of music and musical authorship.

Différance

According to Derrida, *différance* is "neither a word nor a concept" (Derrida 1986: 7). The idiom, which sounds exactly like the French noun *différence* (difference), acquires, through the *é/a* graphic mutation and the addition of the *-ance* suffix, both a verb-inflected dimension, linked to the verb *différer* (to differ), and a new polysemity, difference-differing-deferral. "*Différance* thus designates both a passive difference already in place as the condition of signification and an act of differing which produces differences" (Culler 1982: 97).[16] Furthermore, *différance* aims to connect the differing and deferring aspects involved in the idea of *archi-écriture*, in which signs are never original but part of a chain of endless referral. From that perspective, *différance* allows distinctions without necessarily leading to binary oppositions, stressing heterogeneity yet remaining localized, as it inevitably requires an "answer to the question 'different to what?'" (Hobson 1998: 9). Derrida writes, *différance*:

> is a structure and a movement that cannot be conceived on the basis of the opposition presence/absence. *Différance* is the systematic play of differences, of traces of differences, of the *spacing* by which elements relate to one another. This spacing is the production, simultaneously active and passive (the *a* of *différance* indicates this indecision as regards activity and passivity, that which cannot yet be governed and organized by that opposition), of intervals without which the "full" terms would not signify, would not function.
>
> (Derrida 1981b: 27)

Instead of conceiving of linguistic signs as immediately available, we need to assume that their potential repeatability implies their division *a priori*: their present kernel of meaning is denied in favor of a commitment to past-imposed and future not-yet-existing or "future anterior" meanings. In *Dissemination*, Derrida reflects again on the implications of *différance* from a slightly different perspective:

> *Différance*, the disappearance of any originary presence, is at once the condition of possibility and the condition of impossibility of truth . . . What is, is not what it is, identical and identical to itself, unique, unless it adds to itself the possibility of being repeated as such. And its identity is hollowed out by that addition, withdraws itself in the supplement that presents it. . . . And there is no repetition possible without the graphics of supplementarity.
>
> (Derrida 1981a: 168)

Following the same line of argument, the French thinker, dealing with what Ann Game calls "sociological fictions," explores the presence/absence and real/representation dualisms from an inescapably discursive conception of reality.[17] Derrida points out that the appearance of the "real" depends on its representation, representation becoming a vehicle and precondition that adopts the form of a sign. However, an apparent paradox emerges if we accept the sign-mediated nature of all representations: the real is inevitably permeated with a scarcity, it is deferred, while its representation denies its "real" appearance, which remains mediated, hidden, inaccessible. On the one hand, the sign "represents the present in its absence" and, on the other, "the system (thought or language) [is] governed by and moving toward [an unreachable] presence" (Derrida 1986: 9–10). The presence/absence dualism consequently drifts into an infinite game of deferral and difference, into *différance*.

Marcel Cobussen combines this reading of *différance* and that of arche-writing to develop, in an analysis of the ideas and work of John Cage, the concept of arche-silence: "not a thing, not a presence, but the movement that produces the differences . . . [among] music, sound, noise, and silence. A non-originary origin" (Cobussen 2002: 171). Rose Subotnik invokes as well the notion of *différance* in her deconstructive formulation of a text that is "not identical with itself" (Subotnik 1996: 68). Subotnik's attempt to trace parallelisms between Derridean and Adornian arguments leads Cobussen to ponder the possibility of a formulation of the essence of a musical work as *différance*: "that which makes possible the presentation of the being-present, without ever being presented as such, that which is never offered to the present" (Cobussen 2002: 172). In this light, each interpretation might add new meaning(s) to the text, in a boundless chain, while failing to expose the totality of its multiple intra- and intertextualities. Cobussen's argument is further developed in his analysis – once again – of Gerd Zacher's project *Die Kunst einer Fugue*, where he points out that:

> Music is not a transparent or formal system that banishes ambiguity to be a pure expression of the composer's intentions. To pay tribute to Bach's work means to read his works while bearing in mind the musical accomplishment of our own time. Bach's musical ideas still have power of expression because they were capable of developing; that is to say, they have receded from him in a certain sense. It is precisely by exposing perspectives of his work that Bach could not expose, that we remain loyal to his musical heritage. And disloyal at the same time. Loyalty and disloyalty are interrelated.
>
> (Ibid.: 172)

The Derridean appeal, in *Specters of Marx*, for a radical transformation of the inherited material that exposes the inner resonating elements (Derrida 2006: 18) casts light on the conception of the . . . *Bach* . . . project and its questioning of authorship: the different positions taken by the composers are not alternatives, they do not represent an alienated otherness but are actually embedded in the fabric of Bach's own work. They do not expand the polysemity of Bach's BWV 1002 by adding new isolated meanings but affect its core by perpetuating its ongoing process of *dissemination*, through *différance*, difference-differing-deferral. The compositional model provided by Bach's Partita provides a powerful framework to deliberately expose the inescapability of musical *différance*. But what is presented *prima facie* here attempts, at the same time, to introduce a broader reflection on the nature of all music: it is an exhibition of the inner mechanisms, the entrails, that rest under classical music's perfected façade.

Trace

The notion of *trace* is another key element of Derrida's deconstructive discourse, one characterized by its malleable and complex signification and indebted both to the Heideggerian *Dasein*, to the Freudian *Bahnung*, and to the work and ideas of Emmanuel Lévinas (1906–1995).[18] This *lexeme*, like the others explored in this book, should be understood as an intellectual "organizational pattern" (Hobson 1998: 41) and not as a simple common-use term. In *Of Grammatology*, Derrida defines *trace* as "the temporalization of a lived experience which is neither in the world nor in 'another world'" (Derrida 1976: 65). According to the French philosopher:

> The trace is in fact the absolute origin of sense in general. Which amounts to saying . . . that there is no absolute origin of sense in general. The trace is the differance [sic] which opens appearance . . . and signification. Articulating the living upon the nonliving in general, origin of all repetition, origin of ideality, the trace is not more ideal than real, not more intelligible than sensible, not more a transparent signification than an opaque energy and no concept of metaphysics can describe it.
>
> (Ibid.: 65)

The Derridean trace could also be considered as a structuring structure of infinite referral, one "in which there are only traces – traces prior to any entity of which they might be the trace" (Culler 1982: 99). The author explains, in *Positions*, that:

> [w]hether in written or in spoken discourse, no element can function as a sign without relating to another element which is itself not simply present. This linkage means that each "element" – phoneme or grapheme – is constituted with reference to the trace in it of the other elements of the sequence or system. This linkage, this weaving, is the text, which is produced only through the transformation of another text. Nothing, either in the elements or in the system, is anywhere simply present or absent. There are only, everywhere, differences and traces of traces.
>
> (Derrida 1981b: 37)

As we can see, the notion remains paradoxical within Derrida's own writings. The French thinker asks: "[H]ave I not indefatigably repeated – and would I say demonstrated – that the trace is neither a ground, nor a foundation, nor an origin . . .?" (Derrida 1981b: 51). Derridean trace is thus permeated by a "conceptual" instability, swaying between its bearing as an empirical inscription or mark, the nonpresence of a vanished past, and its vision as a constituent of an ongoing process, through a symbiosis that allows no detachment, separation, or abstraction. Derrida claims that a trace is a "simulacrum of a presence that dislocates itself, displaces itself, refers itself, it properly has no site – erasure belongs to its structure" (Derrida 1986: 24).

Derrida's critical reading of Lévinas, which had a deep influence on his argument, might clarify our present discussion. In an article entitled "The Trace of the Other," originally published in 1963, Lévinas points out that a trace can only be considered as a sign "that signifies outside of every intention of signaling and outside of every project of which it would be the aim" (Lévinas in Taylor 1986: 356–357). The bygone past encapsulated in the trace is irreversible and cannot be disclosed, showcasing what Lévinas defines as the indelibility of being. The signifyingness of a trace, marked by the present/past dualism, doubles the signifyingness proper to signs in general, one exclusively linked to their present bearing. All signs can be seen, as a result, as standing on their traces, which become, under Lévinas's view, "the insertion of space in time, the point at which the world inclines towards a past and a time. This time is a withdrawal of the other, and consequently, nowise a degradation of duration, which, in memory is still complete" (Ibid.: 358).

One further enlightening view of Derridean trace, focused on the centrality of the idea of passage, can be found in Daniel Price's book *Touching Difficulty*. Price explains that "the singularity that has passed, the meaning that has taken shape within our world, can be seen as the key to the structure of passage as such" (Price 2009: 48). Price criticizes the ontotheological view that assumes the necessity of what he terms the "motion of determination," that is, the belief in the ability of traces to reveal a single artificially imposed truth. Instead, he opposes the accessibility of determination: traces will always remain at an unbridgeable distance, since:

> [t]he possibilities arise singularly, like the impossible absences that give the world its shape, that move as the dark "not yet" of the future, without giving it the unity of a single world, or even as an encompassing map of that world . . . the wonder of a singularity that remains, and that sustains a world in the reticent gestures that delay the passage. The beauty is not like a well we draw from, or a resource we exploit, but a site where the passage of the gods is evoked, a form always announced and never merely present, at least where one strives to see the absence, its difficulty. (Ibid.: 249)

Exploring a slightly different approach to the implications of the *lexeme*, Cobussen takes the Derridean trace as a point of departure to conclude that the notion of an original text in music, as in literature, is only the palimpsest of a "pre-text," a text that reflects on its own history, arguing that "any inscription is (only) a trace of former inscriptions" (Cobussen 2002: 15). Cobussen's trace, paralleling Derrida's vision of language as a centerless structure, does not follow a linear teleological pattern. Instead, it connects texts in networks that lack a center, an origin. But if writing becomes a differential trace structure, the closedness of the musical text is consequently refuted, because:

> [a]ny musical "element" functions as a sign, which means that it refers to another element that is simply not present. This connecting chain makes every element of music a constituted beginning with "traces" of other elements of the chain or system within it. This chain is the text, produced only by the way of a transformation of other texts. In other words, a musical work is not identified as the final result of the practice of "creating" music, but as a "mediator" in establishing the chain pointing and indexing events, meanings, senses, and values in relation to other texts.
>
> (Ibid.: 23)

As the textual becomes intertextual, the musical becomes intermusical. In the . . . *Bach* . . . project, the intentional composition of music about music becomes an act of reflection, and the differentiation between music and thinking about music is brought to an end through a "system of differences and traces of traces in which no single musical mark is original nor simply present or absent" (Ibid.: 99). The . . . *Bach* . . . project becomes, in a way, a *mise en abyme*: a work that is reflexive, reflects upon itself, and incorporates that self-reflection.[19]

Coda

In the closing section of Chapter 1, I introduced three critical questions that were left unanswered. They expressed the need to examine the connection between the . . . *Bach* . . . project and the dominant work- and author-concepts. The arguments introduced thus far can now be used to sketch tentative answers, employing some core ideas borrowed from Barthesian and Derridean thinking, which will work both as partially conclusive gestures – drafted in the second Ritornello – and ground, at the same time, the analytical perspectives introduced in Chapter 4.

The conception and structure of the . . . *Bach* . . . project reflect Barthes's claim that literature, as music, is a quagmire where all identity is lost. The project questions the imposition of Bach's authorship as a closing gesture and the idea that Bach's score might release a single teleological reading, both at a compositional level and at a performative level. Bach's text and the contemporary expansions are thus seen as a "tissue of citations," imitating a gesture forever anterior (Barthes 1977: 146). The musical text becomes a *locus* of multiplicity. The new *doubles* traverse Bach's original to generate new levels of meaning, reviving the composer from his Barthesian death.

These new meanings exemplify Derridean *dissémination*, understood as an excess of meaning, an excess that affirms its always divided generation. As I have previously discussed, the . . . *Bach* . . . project becomes a web of recontextualizations, one that, by continuing Bach's original gesture, modifies it: a contamination of authorial subjectivities takes place. Once the dispersion of meaning has escaped the author's (unattainable) intention, the traces that remain as markers of the creative action gain a renewed analytical transcendence, as the following section endeavors to demonstrate, illustrating a process of difference-differing-deferral. The new *doubles* explore the iterability of Bach's compositional gestures, the same iterability that inescapably permeates the isolated features (i.e., authorship markers, stylistic traits) that connect them to the German's music. A new understanding of musical textuality, or should we say musicality, emerges. In . . . *Bach* . . ., the text is expanded, following the Derridean notion of *archi-écriture*, to include most possible referents: context is internalized, discursive thought is internalized, music's own temporality is internalized. The new musical text that emerges from the project's self-reflective act, one that in its uniqueness reflects on the nature of all music, encompasses performative, score-based, aural, and musicological dimensions.

The transcendent ontological focus that permeates most contemporary musicological approaches needs to be contested and reconsidered as well. The issue is not what the musical work *is*; the question is whether the term, given both the conditions of its modern (re)emergence and its historical and metaphysical connotations, is still adequate. I believe that a reading of music and musical textuality that, taking a critical historical perspective, focuses on its absences, on its otherness(es), might provide enlightening alternatives to the ontological approaches explored earlier. This critique might be undertaken, following Derrida's example, by subjecting musical enterprises to a "hauntological" examination. Derrida coins this neologism in *Specters of Marx* to criticize the consideration of the purely positive type of existence, of self-identical presence, introduced by most ontological approaches (Derrida 2006: 10). From a hauntological perspective, according to Mark Fisher, everything that exists can only be seen as "possible on the basis of a whole series of absences, which precede and surround it, allowing it to possess . . . [the] consistency and intelligibility that it does" (Fisher 2014: 18). The idea of a musical hauntology will thus prove to be a useful analytical tool in the ensuing analytical section.

Ritornello II

An exploration of the traces/authorship markers that connect Bach and the contemporary expansions of Buide, Marco, Matamoro, and Järnegard will be the focus of the next chapter. But let us return now to the three fundamental opening questions and introduce some partial answers.

- **Should we consider the . . . *Bach* . . . project as a single work?** I believe that the modern "normative" work-concept cannot be applied to the renewed understanding of musical textuality posited here. Since the . . . *Bach* . . . project is an expansion and continuation of a compositional gesture that lacked a severing act of closure, one that was left partially unfinished – as I believe that all music is – it cannot be attuned to a traditional vision of the work as an *opus perfectum et absolutum*.
- **Who would be its author be? Is there one?** The quasi-theological notion of individual Romantic authorship has also been contested: the . . . *Bach* . . . project, as a form of *archi-écriture*, exemplifies and reveals the intra- and inter-textual dimension of music and the multiplicity of impulses from which all texts emerge. From this perspective, the author becomes a plurality, a divided psyche, possessed by a sort of Hegelian *Geist*.[20]
- **How can these thought-provoking questions help us interrogate and contest the dominant notion of musical authorship? How do they challenge the paradigms permeating the musicological edifice?** The following chapter will introduce analytical case studies that provide a partial answer to this dispute. In them, I expose specific elements – authorship markers – that connect the contemporary expansions to Bach's BWV 1002. Such an analytical approach will further develop and clarify the consideration of Barthesian and Derridean notions undertaken thus far.

Cadential prolongation

Given the condensed nature of the ensuing analyses, the reader would be right to stress that my work here is permeated by an unbalanced relation between interrogation and exegesis. However, I would argue that this is but the logical outcome of the very nature of a novel interpretive approach that does not parallel our traditional understanding of a "deep" score-based examination. Chapter 4 becomes, from that perspective, a concise and transient culminating gesture, a section that outlines analytical paths intended to illuminate the connections between the previous intellectual framework and the specific case studies explored here. The density of the analytical traces is proportional to their briefness: my analytical reflections remain fragmentary, through a specificity that does not necessarily counter, in any case, the coherence of the overall argument, which emerges as a form of discontinuous continuity. I invite the reader to understand them as analytical notes, as inquisitive aphorisms, as pointers and reminders of what remains to be done.

Notes

1 Adam Krims speaks of the "near-epidemic scholarly emulations of the 1970s and 80s, to the at times almost humorous misappropriations in right-wing portrayals of academia, to the popularized usage [of terms like deconstruction], meaning something like critical discussion" (Krims 1998: 298).

2 Significant examples include Snarrenberg (1987), Street (1989), Kramer (1993: 177–215), Littlefield (1996), Scherzinger (1996), Subotnik (1996), Kurth (1997), Hadreas (1999), and Schmidt (2012).

3 Unless we understand musical deconstruction as Cobussen does within the "field of *musical utterance*, that is, the relationship of music towards music" (Cobussen 2002: 4).

4 Hobson borrows the term "strange attractor" from Chaos Theory (Hobson 1998: 107–142). The term is originally used to refer to an apparently random behavior in a nonlinear or chaotic system that is actually characterized by stable nonperiodic patterns.

5 That group would arguably include figures such as Theodor W. Adorno, Edward Said, and Jean-Jacques Nattiez.

6 I argue that these two articles represent a small but telling selection among Barthes's significant output. Another example of a musical-analytical adaptation of the work of the French thinker can be found in an article written by Patrick McCreless, entitled "Roland Barthes's *S/Z* from a Musical Point of View" and originally published in 1988. McCreless traces the potential connections between music and Barthes's *S/Z* by attempting to adapt the five Barthesian narrative codes introduced in *S/Z* (semic, symbolic, referential, proairetic, and hermeneutic) to the Schenkerian analysis of tonal music. I believe that this article exemplifies the kind of imposition of alien intellectual structures that interdisciplinary scholarship should attempt to avoid (see Barthes 1974; Gane 2004: 277–300).

7 The period of civil unrest in Paris in May 1968.

8 One example can be found in the work of the Indian scholar and literary theorist Gayatri Chakravorty Spivak (Spivak 1993: 218).

9 In *S/Z*, Barthes divides Balzac's *Sarrasine* into entities that he terms *lexias* and defines as units of reading that are methodologically arbitrary but large enough to display a limited plurality of meanings. Barthes distinguishes as well between two different regimes of meaning, referring to them as the *texte lisible* or "readerly" and the *texte scriptible* or "writerly." A "readerly" text is one in which the meaning is self-evident while a "writerly" text is one that requires an intellectual effort, its meaning(s) not being easily graspable (Barthes 1974).

10 In a text entitled "This Strange Institution Called Literature" Derrida points out that there is "there is no literature without a *suspended* relation to meaning and reference. Suspended means suspense, but also dependence, condition,

conditionality" (Derrida 1992: 48). Referring to the literary texts that he deals with, he stresses that "the force of their *event* depends on the fact that a thinking about their own possibility (both general and singular) is put to work in them in a singular work . . . texts which are very sensitive to this crisis of the literary institution" (Ibid.: 42).

11 Marcel Cobussen explains, with regard to the possibility of a musical parasitism, that in music:

> there is always room for parasitism because of an openness in the interior . . . a possibility available in the materiality of the music itself. No (musical) text is closed upon itself. The possibility of parasitism – parasitism regarded as (mis)use, quotation, or imitation, i. e. repeating and presenting the music in a different context – is always present.
>
> (Cobussen 2002: 101)

12 Examples of performative utterances being "I do . . . ," "I give . . . ," "I hereby . . . ." (Austin 1962: 60–61).

13 Derrida introduces the notion of seal here as a metaphorical representation of signature. The seal epitomizes the physicality of the signature as that wax or material that serves as a guarantor of authenticity. The tension that emerges from the contradictory conditions of the effects and nature of signature divide, according to Derrida, the seal from within.

14 The conception of the signature as a reflexive short-circuit, as a kind of *mise en abyme* or signature of the signature, is expressed by Derrida on the following terms:

> [W]e may designate as general signature, or signature of the signature, the fold of the placement in abyss, where after the manner of the signature in the current sense, the work of writing designates, describes, and inscribes itself as act (action and archive), signs itself before the end by affording us the opportunity to read: I refer to myself, this is writing, I am writing, this is writing – which excludes *nothing* since, when the placement in abyss succeeds, and is thereby decomposed and produces an event, it is the other, the thing as other, that signs.
>
> (Derrida 1984: 54)

15 This is clearly exemplified in Plato's *Phaedrus*. Socrates, discussing the rules of speech and writing, tells Phaedrus that:

> writing shares a strange feature with painting. The offsprings of painting stand there as if they are alive, but if anyone asks them anything, they remain most solemnly silent. The same is true of written words. You'd think they were speaking as if they had some understanding, but if you question anything that has been said because you want to learn more, it continues to signify just that very same thing forever. When it has once been written down, every discourse roams about everywhere, reaching indiscriminately those with understanding no less than those who have no business with it, and it doesn't know to whom it should speak and to whom it should not. And when it is faulted and attacked unfairly, it always needs its father's support; alone, it can neither defend itself nor come to its own support.
>
> (Cooper 1997: 552)

16 Derrida refers to the letter *a* of *différance* as the "inaudible misplacement of... [a] literal permutation" (Derrida 1986: 3). *Différance* parallels the English term "spacing," used by Derrida sometimes on its French version *espacement* in his text and borrowed once again from Mallarmé. See the typographical play in Mallarmé's poem *Un coup de dés* as an example of the employment of the white space as a textual element (Mallarmé 2006: 161–181).

17 In her book *Undoing the Social*, Ann Game attempts to transcend "sociological fictions," the traditional sociological distinctions between representation/real, text/context, theory/practice. Her deconstructive approach challenges sociology to accept the real as fiction and fiction as reality. In order to do so, the discipline needs to assume that it is not self-identical with:

> the objects that it discursively proposes. A project of undoing consists, then, in destabilizing the givenness of objects; and an initial move in this is to demonstrate the ways in which objects or the social are constituted in order to return to the subject of sociology.
>
> (Game 1991: 20)

18 *Bahnung* (breaching) had been used by the Russian physiologist Ivan Pavlov to refer to the creation of neurological paths that were repeatedly excited simultaneously. Freud adopted the term to refer to the process of formation of unconscious memory in his *Project for a Scientific Psychology* (Freud 1966: 295–398). The Heideggerian *Dasein*, which translates as being-there or being-in-the-world, relates to the study of the human in all its ways of being (Derrida 1978: 196–231, 1987). For an introduction to Lévinas's ideas, see Michael Morgan's *The Cambridge Introduction to Emmanuel Levinas* (Morgan 2011).

19 *Mise en abyme* refers here to a recursive type of self-contained art. Marian Hobson points out that "in literary theory, with the mise en abyme as a series of reflections or internally contained scale-models of the literary work, such doubles might give consistency and coherence to the literary or pictural [or musical] work by encapsulating images which reflect the whole, by reinforcing and repeating it" (Hobson 1998: 75).

20 In this case, I refer to its understanding as a sort of "general consciousness, a single 'mind' common to all men" (Solomon 1970: 642).

References

Austin, John L. *How to Do Things with Words*. New York: Oxford University Press, 1962.

Barthes, Roland. *S/Z*. New York: Hill & Wang, 1974.

———. *The Pleasure of the Text*. New York: Hill & Wang, 1975.

———. *Image-Music-Text*. New York: Hill & Wang, 1977.

———. *Sade, Fourier, Loyola*. Berkeley: University of California Press, 1989.

Burke, Seán. *The Death and Return of the Author: Criticism and Subjectivity in Barthes, Foucault and Derrida*. Edinburgh: Edinburgh University Press, 1992.

Cobussen, Marcel. "Deconstruction in Music." PhD diss., Erasmus University Rotterdam, 2002.

Cooper, John M., ed. *Plato: Complete Works*. Indianapolis, IN: Hackett Publishing Company, 1997.

Culler, Jonathan. *On Deconstruction: Theory and Criticism after Structuralism*. Ithaca, NY: Cornell University Press, 1982.

Derrida, Jacques. *Of Grammatology*. Baltimore: Johns Hopkins University Press, 1976.

———. *Writing and Difference*. Chicago: University of Chicago Press, 1978.

———. *Dissemination*. Chicago: University of Chicago Press, 1981a.

———. *Positions*. Chicago: University of Chicago Press, 1981b.

———. *Signéponge/Signsponge*. New York: Columbia University Press, 1984.

———. *Margins of Philosophy*. Chicago: University of Chicago Press, 1986.

———. *Of Spirit: Heidegger and the Question*. Chicago: University of Chicago Press, 1987.

———. *Acts of Literature*. New York: Routledge, 1992.

———. *Limited Inc*. Evanston, IL: Northwestern University Press, 1997.

———. *Specters of Marx: The State of the Debt, the Work of the Mourning and the New International*. New York: Routledge, 2006.

Fisher, Mark. *Ghosts of My Life: Writings on Hauntology, Depression, and Lost Futures*. Washington, DC: Zero Books, 2014.

Freud, Sigmund. *The Standard Edition of the Complete Psychological Works of Sigmund Freud, Volume I (1886–1899): Pre-Psycho-Analytic Publications and Unpublished Drafts*. London: Hogarth Press and the Institute of Psycho-Analysis, 1966.

Game, Ann. *Undoing the Social: Towards a Deconstructive Sociology*. Toronto: University of Toronto Press, 1991.

Gane, Mike, and Nicholas Gane, eds. *Roland Barthes*, Vol. 2. Thousand Oaks, CA: Sage Publications Inc., 2004.

Hadreas, Peter. "Deconstruction and the Meaning of Music." *Perspectives of New Music* 37, no. 2 (Summer 1999): 5–28.

Hill, Leslie. *The Cambridge Introduction to Derrida*. New York: Cambridge University Press, 2007.

Hobson, Marian. *Jacques Derrida: Opening Lines*. New York: Routledge, 1998.

Kramer, Lawrence. *Music as Cultural Practice 1800–1900*. Berkeley: University of California Press, 1993.

Krims, Adam. "Disciplining Deconstruction (For Music Analysis)." *19th-Century Music* 21, no. 3 (Spring 1998): 297–324.

Kurth, Richard. "Music and Poetry, a Wilderness of Doubles: Heine-Nietzsche-Schubert-Derrida." *19th-Century Music* 21, no. 2 (1997): 3–37.

Littlefield, Richard. "The Silence of the Frames." *Music Theory Online* 2, no. 1 (January 1996).

Mallarmé, Stéphane. *Collected Poems and Other Verse*. New York: Oxford University Press, 2006.

Morgan, Michael L. *The Cambridge Introduction to Emmanuel Levinas*. New York: Cambridge University Press, 2011.

Price, Daniel M. *Touching Difficulty: Sacred from Plato to Derrida*. Aurora, CO: Davies Group Publishers, 2009.

Scherzinger, Martin. "The Finale of Mahler's Seventh Symphony: A Deconstructive Reading." *Music Analysis* 14 (1996): 69–88.

Schmidt, Patrick. "What We Hear Is Meaning Too: Deconstruction, Dialogue, and Music." *Philosophy of Music Education Review* 20, no. 1 (Spring 2012): 3–24.

Snarrenberg, Robert. "The Play of Différance: Brahms Intermezzo, Op. 118, No. 2." *In Theory Only* 10 (October 1987): 1–25.

Solomon, Robert C. "Hegel's Concept of Geist." *The Review of Metaphysics* 23, no. 4 (1970): 642–661.

Spivak, Gayatri Chakravorty. *Outside in the Teaching Machine*. New York: Routledge, 1993.

Street, Alan. "Superior Myths, Dogmatic Allegories: The Resistance to Musical Unity." *Music Analysis* 8 (1989): 77–123.

Subotnik, Rose. *Deconstructive Variations: Music and Reason in Western Society*. Minneapolis: University of Minnesota Press, 1996.

Taylor, Mark C. *Deconstruction in Context: Literature and Philosophy*. Chicago: University of Chicago Press, 1986.

4 Death and (re)birth of J. S. Bach

Case studies[1]

Methodological considerations: authorship markers

In this section I explore the iterability of Bach's compositional gestures in the BWV 1002, conceived here as authorship markers, from a music-analytical perspective. Four *doubles* from the . . . *Bach* . . . project that expand each of the four main dance movements are employed as case studies: Fernando Buide's *Doble* on the Allemande, Miguel Matamoro's *(. . .)* on the Corrente, Tomas Marco's *Double de Double* on the Sarabande, and Esaias Järnegard's *Ymagino* on the Tempo di Borea. These analyses examine the commonalities of their musical fabrics under the enlightening intellectual world that emerges from a critical approach to Barthes's and Derrida's writings, applying those notions, organizational patterns, or "circuits of argument" considered thus far.

The most important assumption underpinning the ensuing analyses, the application of the intellectual framework developed in the preceding chapter, and the arguments raised in the book's final concluding gesture is the fundamental connection between the ideas of trace and authorship marker. I believe that a further clarification of this linkage is necessary here and that a consideration of another Derridean *lexeme*, that of *restance*, familially connected to the notions of "trace" and "iterability," might enlighten such clarification. *Restance* is a neologism derived from the French verb *rester* (to remain) that refers as well to the noun *reste* (remainder).[2] Derrida provides a basic definition in *Limited Inc*, where he identifies *restance* as the minimal possibility of reusing a sign: "the remainder is . . . bound up with the minimal possibility of the re-mark . . . and with the structure of iterability" (Derrida 1988: 53). Among a broader examination of the intellectual implications of Derridean *restance* that stresses some of the ideas discussed in the preceding consideration of iterability, Marian Hobson argues that "the very possibility of recontextualizing, or of fictionalizing . . . renders stability of essence impossible. Its implication of both identity and difference is not just a fact – that any instance of repetition is a different instance from the preceding one, even if the instances are 'identical'" (Hobson 1998: 100). Thus the possibility of repetition, considered as the basic precondition of language, grounds the apparently paradoxical inescapability of both identity and difference. When considered through Derridean *restance*, a linguistic element loses the "presentness" of its meaning and becomes a working "through commitments of meaning which the past continually imposes and which arise from what will be the future's effect" (Ibid.: 107). Derrida argues that "iterability supposes a minimal remainder [*reste*] . . . in order that the identity of the *selfsame* be repeatable and identifiable *in*, *through*, and even *in view* of its alteration" (Derrida 1988: 53). *Restance* is a minimal point of adherence, in which, as Hobson points out, "the single occurrence and its repetition, in other words singularity and iterability, can 'fall together,' that is, coincide, pulling into existence something that like certain sorts of mathematical limits, can be formulated, approached as closely as one likes, but not made present" (Hobson 1998: 117). Derridean *restance* thus brings together, into an analytic-intellectual cluster or constellation, the notions of "trace" and "authorship marker."

Following the previous argument, we now come to realize how the authorship markers explored in the ensuing section serve an analytical purpose but cannot be seen as frozen or ossified formulations. They are embedded in the idea of Derridean *différance* and, as such, are not reducible to an ontologically or teleologically organized discourse, since "there is nowhere to *begin* the sheaf or the graphics of *différance*" (Derrida 1986b: 6). Authorship markers, like Derridean *restance*, have to be understood as dynamic, as moving. As traces, they remain at a distance, inaccessible, paralleling Derrida's opaque energy. From Lévinas's perspective, they represent the insertion of space in time, the point at which music inclines toward a past and a time that becomes a withdrawal of the other.

Authorship markers underpin as well a general fetishization of the composer's name, one similarly fashioned in the . . . *Bach* . . . project to those on Derrida's *Signsponge*, a pun on the name of the French poet Francis Ponge, or Barthes's *Sade, Fourier, Loyola*. That fetishization and its relation to what could be defined as the epitome of the author-function, as a "signer," "namer," or "appropriator," open a potential path for a sociopolitical level of critique, one that will nonetheless be left unexplored here. In the . . . *Bach* . . . project, Bach's name goes beyond its role as a proper name to describe or designate, to generate a more complex referential structure. Its fetishization can be thus linked to the Derridean "phantasm" and "specter," ideas that play a key role on the French thinker's exploration of the ghostly dimension of the fetish.[3] A similar approach is articulated in *Glas*, amid a critical commentary on Freud's *Beyond the Pleasure Principle* (Freud 1990). Derrida introduces there a vision of the fetish as a link between two contraries, the "real thing" and its "fetishized" substitute. The French thinker points out that

> The fetish's consistency, resistance, remnance [*restance*], is in proportion to its undecidable bond to contraries. Thus the fetish – in general – begins to exist only as it begins to bind itself to contraries. So this double bond, this double ligament, defines its subtlest structure. All the consequences of this must be drawn. The economy of the fetish is more powerful than that of the truth – decidable – of the thing itself or than a deciding discourse of castration (*pro aut contra*). The fetish is not opposable. It oscillates like the clapper of a truth that rings awry [*cloche*].
>
> (Derrida 1986a: 227)

Derrida's vision of the fetish as a "double bond" provides a powerful framework to reassess the analytical transcendence of the authorship markers: the fetish's *restance*, its consistency and resistance, can be linked to its role as a ligament that "undecidably" unites these apparent contraries. Authorship markers hence represent an analytical approach to the structure of that connective tissue, of that ligament.

One further reading of the fetishization undertaken by the . . . *Bach* . . . project can be made under a Barthesian perspective. Barthes employs the term, like Derrida, from a Freudian approach to designate "the solution to the split between what we know intellectually and what we desire" (Gallop 2011: 31). According to Barthes, the text is a fetish object that desires the reader, while the reader, wandering in the desiring textual object, inevitably longs for the return of the bygone author, since:

> [t]he text chooses me, by a whole disposition of invisible screens, selective baffles: vocabulary, references, readability, etc.; and, lost in the midst of a text (not behind it, like a *deus ex machina*) there is always the other, the author.
>
> (Barthes 1998: 27)

From such perspective, the . . . *Bach* . . . project showcases a desire for a return that is already negated by the ellipses that precede and follow the German composer's name; the project thus becomes a rhetorical search for the nonexistent, for the already-denied.

When, in the opening lines of the present book, I defined authorship markers as elements that reveal the traces of Bach's compositional gestures, I also acknowledged that, by exploring such features, I was attempting to reflect on a process introduced here as an overt given – thus the nature and conception of the . . . *Bach* . . . project – but that nonetheless permeates all music. Bach is not a point of departure; Bach is only selected as an incision on the ongoingness of a preceding and expanding trace-structure. Bach is a "posibilitator" both of a compositional space and of a resultant arena within which listening can happen, a territory that might be modified without being necessarily abandoned by other composers. That being said, the . . . *Bach* . . . project is not a simple imitation or a reappropriation of the German's music: even through its suprahistorical critique – the reconsideration of the dominant work- and author-concepts – it remains historically located by positing a musical reflection on Bach's role as a cornerstone of the Western classical music tradition.

Bach/Buide: new dice, an old game[4]

As we have seen, in its simplest form, a *double* can be defined as a re-elaboration of the figured bass of the preceding dance movement. Fernando Buide's extension of Bach's original takes this strict reading as a point of departure. The Allemande's figured bass (see Example 4.1) is used as a basis for a variation that explores, through Buide's personal approach, Bach's characteristic technique of horizontal polyphony. A comparison between the harmonies of the Allemande (see Example 4.2 and Video 1) and those of Buide's *Doble* (see Example 4.3 and Video 2) shows that, in the opening measures, Buide rarely departs from Bach's harmonic framework (nonharmonic notes are marked in gray).

Example 4.1 J. S. Bach BWV 1002, Allemande, figured bass[5]

Example 4.2 J. S. Bach BWV 1002, Allemande, harmonies, opening measures

Example 4.3 F. Buide, *Doble*, harmonies, opening measures

Albeit the untouched harmonic structure, Buide explores two key elements that reflect upon and partially digress from Bach's example. First, as I mentioned earlier, the Spanish composer introduces a form of horizontal polyphony characterized by broader and more continuous registral shifts. The performer seems to be looking at Bach through a shattered glass. Chart 4.1 (see following) includes a graphic representation of Buide's *Doble* that depicts time in seconds against a vertical disposition of pitch, measured in hertz (Hz) (Example 4.4, which corresponds to Video 3, introduces an alternative score-based depiction of this horizontal polyphony).[6] Looking both at the distance between contiguous sound-events and at the horizontal lines that emerge in the overall picture, we can get a visually clear impression of the continuity of register changes and the underpinning structure of horizontal polyphony. Buide's music departs from Bach's example in a second fundamental aspect: two fragments introduce an organic increase of rhythmic activity that resemble the kind of "improvised" embellished ornamental section typical of a baroque solo sonata or fugal episode, introducing a form of inner elaboration, a *double*-within-the-*double* (see Example 4.5 and Video 4).

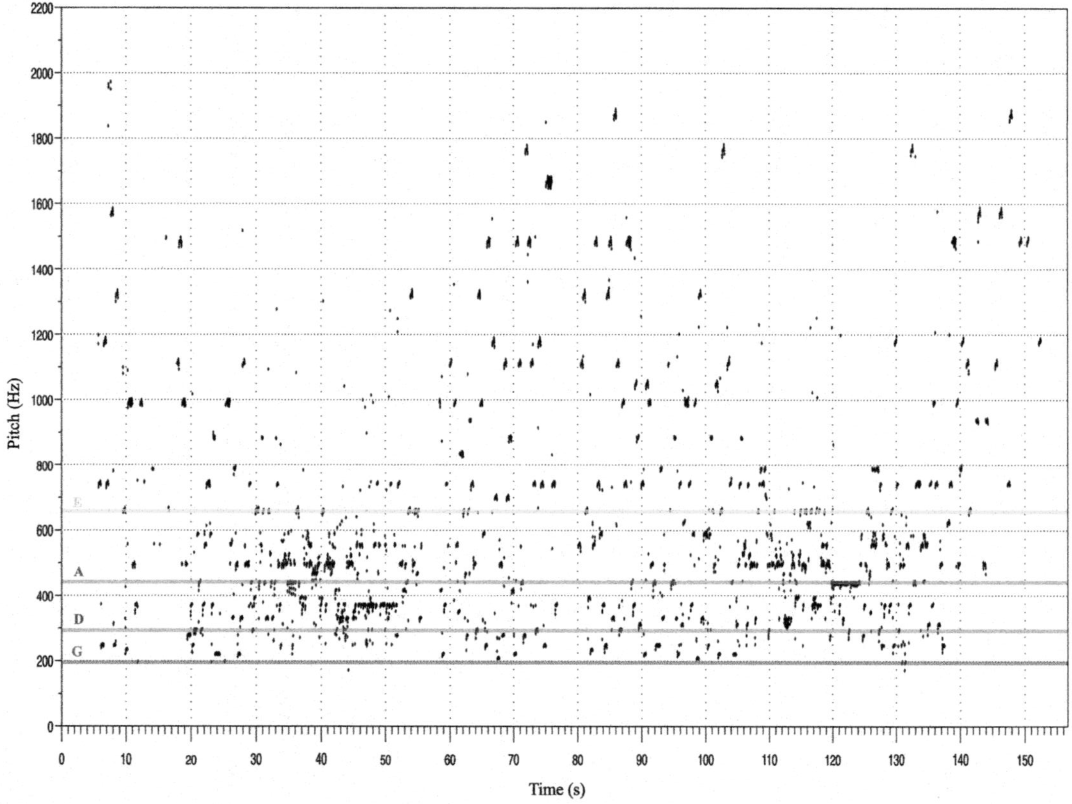

Chart 4.1 Fernando Buide, *Doble*, pitch chart

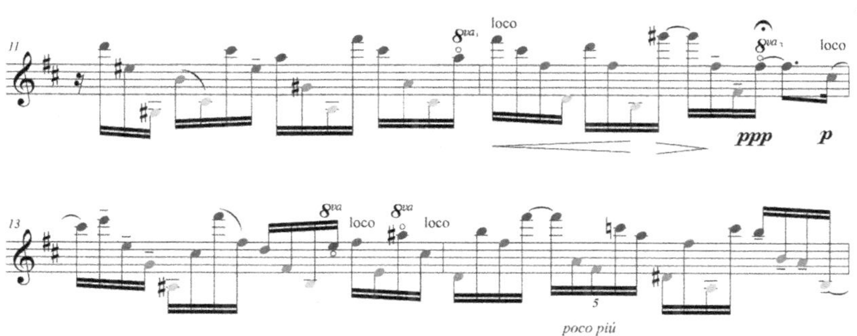

Example 4.4 F. Buide, *Doble*, horizontal polyphony, mm. 11–14

Example 4.5 F. Buide, *Doble*, double-within-the-double, mm. 5–7

A Derridean game of *différance* seems to be taking place. Bach is perceived as an absent presence, while Buide is not fully there, his music openly avoiding self-referentiality. Each musical element is "constituted on the basis of the trace within it of the other elements of the chain or system. This interweaving, this textile, is the text produced only in the transformation of another text" (Derrida 1981b: 26). Buide brings Bach back from his Barthesian death; his vital impulse having been transplanted from his "same/iter" (ego) to a certain form of "otherness" (text ↔ score ↔ performer ↔ listener). Furthermore, as Derrida points out, if *différance* intervenes, all the conceptual oppositions that permeate and ground traditional metaphysics become nonpertinent. *Différance* negates the possibility of a precursory meaning, what Derrida defines as the "transcendental signified," a signified that represents a conception of the author's original intention that might exceed or govern textual or musical formulation.[7] Buide's *Doble* thus posits a powerful example of intra-/intertextuality that questions the author-god figure and Romantic subjectivity and makes necessary a reading of the text outside-the-text, that is, the expansion, once again, of musical textuality. The listener-performer becomes the *locus* where that textual multiplicity is pulled together, and the vision of the author as a *deus-ex-machina* vanishes. As Derrida would put it:

> He who says I in the present, in the so-called positive event constituted by his discourse, would be capable of only an illusion of mastery. At the very moment he thinks he is directing the operations, his place – the opening toward the present assumed by whoever believes himself capable of saying I, I think, I am, I see, I feel, I say . . . is . . . being decided by a throw of dice whose law will subsequently be developed inexorably by chance.
>
> (Derrida 1981b: 298)

> FB: . . . writing music after another composer implies setting forth a reading of the original score. In a way, composing the Double becomes, at the same time, an attempt to explain my reading of Bach. The elements in Bach's music that I find more powerfully resonant become the basis that grounds my new gesture, my "differánce." Barthes shifts the role of creating meaning to the reader: I produce instead a new text, as a reader/writer, that emerges from the process of subjectively finding and creating meaning from/through/within Bach's music. But the process of creating a new piece stemming from Bachian elements implies breaking away from the role of author – the player and listener must now assume such position. The importance given to the harmonic structure, the idea of a dense polyphonic web, the Baroque notion of rhythmic variation and acceleration are several of the parameters that help me discover the logic in Bach's music narrative; those elements are the basis that articulates my own musical proposal . . .

Buide's *Doble* parallels the twenty-four-measure structure of Bach's Allemande and Bach's original Double. The re-elaboration of the figured bass is maintained throughout. Nevertheless, Bach's *restance* renders Buide's music unstable, and, as a result, the music fails to come to an end,

Example 4.6 F. Buide, *Doble*, ending, mm. 21–24

to conclude. Instead, Buide's *Doble* collapses, it disintegrates into a void (see Example 4.6 and Video 5). The previously explored twofoldness of the Derridean trace allows us to understand Buide's music as an exemplification of Daniel Price's discussion of passage: the accessibility of Bach's compositional gestures is ultimately denied in spite of Buide's reflectively connective incisions on the processual traces of the German's music. Buide's music becomes, following Derrida, a simulacrum of a present that takes place under its own erasure (Price 2009: 248).

Bach/Matamoro: Bach as movement/Bach as gesture[8]

Miguel Matamoro's continuation of Bach's original, entitled *(. . .)*, introduces an element of irony that can be explored from an etymological perspective, paralleling Derrida's fascination.[9] The French term *double* evolves from the Latin *duplus*, the addition of the idioms *duo* (two) and *plus* (more) (Barnhart 1988: 297). As we have seen, *double* refers to a variation movement, within the Baroque suite, that applies the division/diminution techniques. Bach's original Double for the Corrente is a long and technically demanding motto-perpetuo marked presto (see Example 4.7). Matamoro, given the lively tempo of the Corrente and the standard set by Bach's Double, inverts the compositional pattern: the rhythmic values are extended, instead of compressed, and the *double* becomes a *medius*, a *moyen* (see Example 4.8 and Video 6). Matamoro only introduces the expected duplicity/duplication after the opening section reverts the Corrente to a nonexisting dance – the Corrente becoming the *double* of the new expansive gesture – eventually relocating Bach's music in its expected referential position as source and not as elaboration. Matamoro's *(. . .)* thus relates to the ellipses that both precede and follow Bach in the project's title.

Example 4.7 J. S. Bach, BWV 1002, *Double*, opening measures

Example 4.8 M. Matamoro, *(. . .)*, mm. 1–7

> MM: . . . personally, I am interested in anything that is relatable: the observation and the analysis of such relationships is, to my understanding, the essence of the creative work . . . When I speak about relationships I am referring to the idea as such, with no further bearings: observing the connections between objects/bodies/ideas without ever intending to abandon, to move beyond, such a level of analysis. It is there that my search emerges, it barely focuses on the individuality of the elements to find a reality of interconnected objects/bodies/ideas that configures, in essence, my imaginary. It is a network of endless connections, a tissue of circuits that unites each ipseity to configure the "work." In each connection you might be able to find essential clues that enlighten your understanding of art; that is, from my point of view, what the study of music is about . . .

Two key authorship markers connect Bach and Matamoro's music, two markers that expose traces of the network of relatable elements that shape Matamoro's compositional imaginary. First, Matamoro's expansion grasps the essence of the gestural dimension of Bach's music, even if the aural outcome is remarkably different. But what do I mean by gestural dimension? The study of gestuality in music has been undertaken from diverse perspectives, including its examination as embodied meaning, as bodily metaphors, its consideration from motor and neurological perspectives as well as from a visual-analytical approach.[10] Scholars Marc Leman and Rolf Inge Godøy propose the following basic definition, a definition that in spite of its simplicity will ground my ensuing argument: a gesture is a "movement of a part of the body . . . to express an idea or meaning" (Leman and Godøy 2010: 5). I believe that the gestural is only partially conveyed in the notated score: its broader consideration has to emerge from an understanding of the musical text that goes, under an expanded relatability, beyond the purely semiotic. Identical rhythmic and pitch combinations will imply and require a different gestuality in Bach, Brahms, and Stockhausen. The gestural becomes one further location of meaning that expands music's textuality. But how can such a specific understanding of gestuality be explained? The performer's own bodily perception plays an important role: this first-person perspective, as defined by Marc Leman, makes possible a vision of music as "performed and perceived through gestures whose deployment can be directly felt and understood through the body, without the need of verbal descriptions" (Ibid.: 127). Those gestures reveal the textuality of performance and thus render their verbalization unnecessary. Hence, in order to avoid a biased translation, I will let the reader attempt to grasp and recreate my view by examining two videos that include a gesture-focused rendition of the Corrante and of Matamoro's expansion: Video 7 presents a split-screen simultaneous interpretation of Bach's original, on the left-hand side, and Matamoro's on the right. Both videos are first introduced without audio to exclusively focus on their performative gestuality: Bach's music can be seen here a gestural duplication of Matamoro's while Matamoro's gestuality emerges from elements found in Bach's slower opening Allemande or in the following Sarabande. A second version of the same material mutes only Bach's Corrente before a final repetition dampens Matamoro's *(. . .)*, exposing all the gestural relationships that emerge between both *doubles*.

Such a first-person analysis of the gestural leads to a second element that connects Bach's original to Matamoro's music. In order to clarify my argument, I would like to tangentially examine an Adornian discussion of music as movement, as embodied dance, music understood as a metakinetic elaboration. Through the application of the polysemic notion of *bewegung*,

Theodor W. Adorno refers to one of Beethoven's symphonies in the following terms:[11]

> The relationship of the symphony to dance may be defined as follows: if dance appeals to the bodily movements of human beings, then the symphony is the music that itself becomes a body . . . the totality of its gestures is the intentionless representation of the body . . . this corporeal nature of the symphony is its social essence: it is the giant body, the collective body of society in the dialectic of its moments.
>
> (Adorno 1998: 262)

If music can be seen as codified and sublimated movement, Matamoro's exploration of the gestural as an authorship marker propels his music back to a reflective presublimated phase, a form of proto-archi-writing: movement thus becomes the essential condition of music. What lies at the core of the historical origin of the suite/partita is its role as musical accompaniment to, and musical elaboration of, dance movements. Its later stylization, in an exploration of music's own idiomatic possibilities, led to the development of the Baroque suite as exemplified in Bach's BWV 1002. Following Barthes, Matamoro dives into the music, bypassing Bach's authoriality to return it to a pre-Bachian dimension/space, exploring a pre-textual aspect that connects both.

Matamoro introduces into this process of exploration a further element that can be enlightened by a Derridean reading. His music lives in the awareness of its trace-nature. The composer plays among three different sound-worlds, indicated throughout as *legno tratto* – playing with the wooden part of the bow, *legno e crine* – playing with both wood and horsehair, and *crine* – use the bow standardly with full horsehair (see Example 4.9 and Video 8). These sound-worlds represent an otherness that flourishes within the space that Bach "possibilitates." The use of "standard" sound is confined to a few sections. The work thus recreates a sonic space that presents the performer as failing to unearth a gesture that is never fully defined, always blurred, never uncovered: music as trace, "nothing . . . is anywhere simply present or absent. There are only, everywhere, differences and traces of traces" (Derrida 1981b: 37). Consequently, Matamoro's music can be seen part of the *mise en abyme* that the game-of-doubles of the . . . *Bach* . . . project represents: it is an exposed reflection on the nature of music as creation and mediation, a *cogitant* trace that, with a probing attitude, reflects from within the textual space on the intertextual nature of its own existence.

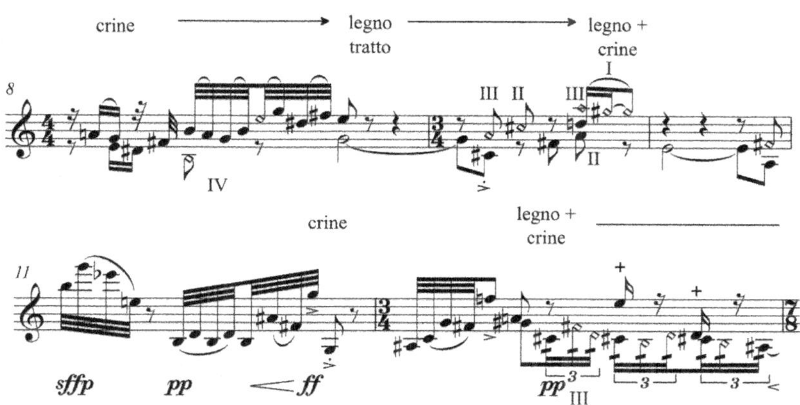

Example 4.9 M. Matamoro, *(. . .)*, mm. 8–12, bow techniques

> MM: . . . the imaginary works the same way. When we speak about imagination we are actually referring to the possible or to that distance that emerges with the reality that we choose to inhabit. To put it differently, we move between reality and the limits of the impossible, the outcome of that experience being the imagined. The significance of a "contemporary attitude" lies precisely on the ability to imagine from the present reality . . . The basic principle of the "contemporary" is that it immediately stops being so; the "contemporary" is a constant, there cannot be contemporaneity without a searching attitude . . . .

Bach/Marco: Bach's signature[12]

Bach initiates all the movements of his BWV 1002, aside from the Corrente, with the same chord in root position and with similar finger dispositions (see Example 4.10).[13] This chord is thus employed as a tonal marker that unites the Partita as a coherent whole. Tomás Marco's expansion of the Sarabande transforms this element into a repeated structural anchoring gesture, one that provides a sense of punctuation, of verticality, to rather fluid connective material. Bach's tonal marker is repeated a total of twenty-one times (see Chart 4.2 following).[14]

Example 4.10 J. S. Bach, BWV 1002, opening chords of Allemanda, Sarabande, and Tempo di Borea

The B minor chord can be seen, as well as Bach's signature and Marco's repetition, as an exploration of its different meanings. Derrida points out that a:

> written signature implies the actual or empirical nonpresence of the signer . . . it also marks and retains his having-been present in a past now, which will remain a future now, and therefore in a now in general, in the transcendental of nowness (maintenance). This general maintenance is somehow inscribed, stapled to present punctuality, always evident and always singular, in the form of the signature . . . [D]oes the absolute singularity of an event of signature ever occur? . . . [T]he condition of possibility for these effects [of signature] is simultaneously, once again, the condition of their impossibility, of the impossibility of the rigorous purity.
>
> (Derrida 1986b: 328)

In this light, Marco, through this reiteration, brings Bach back from his Barthesian death before he returns the German composer, through a dislocation of the gesture, to a spectral level. The iteration of the signature eventually leads, by dint of a process of continuous recontextualizations, to a questioning of the transcendental nowness that it might have insinuated on its first appearance. Bach's signature loses its identity and becomes Marco's own.

This *Double de Double* explores as well other dimensions of musical iterability, which, as Cobussen argued, is "always inscribed in the functional structure of the musical mark" (Cobussen 2002: 46). Marco seems to focus on repetitive structural aspects of the baroque style that abound in Bach's music but are not necessarily present in this Sarabande (think of fugal or extensive sequential writing). For example, Marco reiteratively repeats different combinations of Bach's opening harmonic progression (see Example 4.11 and Video 9) up to three times in the first six measures of his expansion (see Example 4.12 and Video 10). The signature chords are followed by an

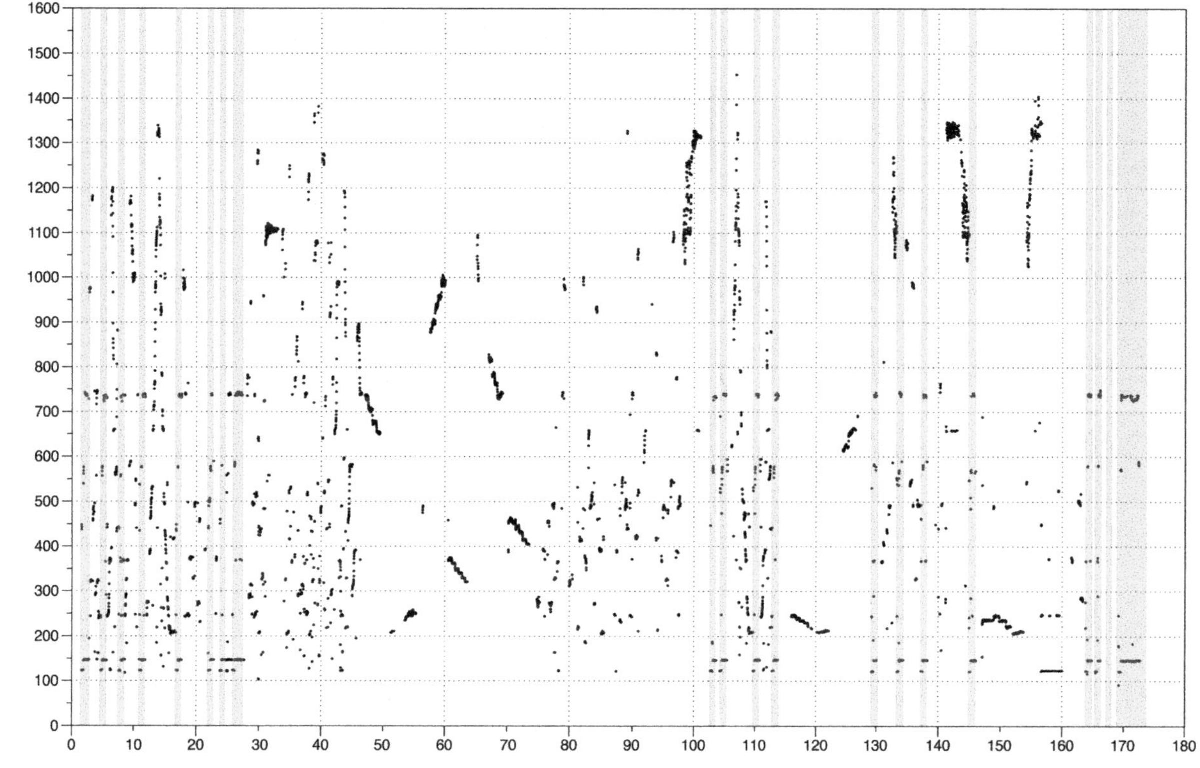

Chart 4.2 Tomás Marco, *Double de Double*, pitch versus chord chart

Example 4.11 J. S. Bach, BWV 1002, Sarabande, harmonies of the opening measures

Example 4.12 T. Marco, *Double de Double*, harmonies, mm. 1–6

implied supertonic marked in red, a repetition of the tonic marked in blue, and an implied dominant marked in yellow. Through the employment of these repetitive structures the *Double de Double* delves into the compositional territory "possibilitated" by Bach, letting both the performer and the listener ramble in the listening space that emerges from/through his music, a space that might be modified but that is never abandoned in Marco's continuation. This appropriation of the "possibilitated" space involves an element of violence as well, an incisive countering of the received that represents a form of withdrawal, a tearing of the inherited fabric that always remains partial, wanting.

TM: . . . my reading of Bach's Sarabande takes both the basic generative chord and the structure of Bach's whole BWV 1002 as a point of departure. I subjected the signature chord to a series of different transformations. Such a process stands on an ambiguous relationship with Bach's original, one of approximation and estrangement . . .

The following section of Marco's *Double* takes the focus on iteration to an even further level, exploring elements of set theory (see Example 4.13, Video 11 and Table 4.1). Measures sixteen to twenty introduce a full twelve-tone row, which is reduced to eleven pitches, and eventually ten in the three following rows. All the rows are connected by the partial inverted iteration of pitch-sequences that, like examples of learned style, generate a sense of baroque-like interplay.

The overall structure of Marco's *Double de Double* involves another form of iteration: it is constructed through the continuous reemployment of motivic material. Nonetheless, after the thirty-two opening measures that correspond to the full length of Bach's original Sarabande, Marco's music takes an unexpected turn: the composer introduces a slower Moderato tempo and longer note values to present small rising and descending

Example 4.13 T. Marco, *Double de Double*, mm. 17–29

Table 4.1 T. Marco, *Double de Double*, pitch sequence, mm. 16–29

I	mm. 16-20	{7, 2, 10, 11, 6, 0, 3, 8, 9, 4, 5, 1}
II	mm. 21-23	{1, 5, 4, 8, 3, 0, 6, 11, 7, 9, 2}
III	mm. 24-26	{2, 10, 7, 6, 0, 3, 8, 9, 4, 5, 1}
IV	mm. 27-29	{5, 4, 11, 3, 0, 6, 9, 1, 2, 7}

Example 4.14 T. Marco, *Double de Double*, quarter tones, mm. 33–39

intervals divided into quarter-tone steps (see Example 4.14 and Video 12). The music seems to be unable to advance at the same pace, to keep on re-elaborating Bach's traces. An element of apparent resistance emerges, pointing to the tension that results from the fetishization of the German's music that the . . . *Bach* . . . project enacts: the ligament that unites, through the Derridean "double bond," the real and its substitute acquires a vacillating tension that discloses, over a temporal glimpse, those connective traces that the authorship markers and Derridean *restance* represent.

> TM: . . . I have attempted to introduce a timbric-harmonic elaboration that is, at the same time, a response to the featured instrument, the violin. There is an employment of "the baroque" that emerges, simultaneously, from its own space and from a contemporary reading . . . I introduce the use of repetition in a way that allows the music to establish a subtle multi-layered interplay between identity, similarity, and their endless intermediate degrees . . .

Bach/Järnegard: Bach as space/Bach as sound[15]

Esaias Järnegard's personal exploration and unique conception of sound connects his *double* to Bach's original Tempo di Borea. Järnegard conceptualizes sound not as a purely abstract dimension of music (i.e., pitch, dynamic level, texture) but as a physically resonating reality, one that is necessarily linked to an idealized reverberating space. The following question arises: how can such an understanding of the inner spatiality of music be reflected in the conception of this specific *double*? The ensuing analysis of Järnegard's contribution to the . . . *Bach* . . . project attempts to find an answer to that question and introduces further enlightening examples of the application of specific elements of Barthesian and Derridean thinking to music.

EJ: . . . how is it possible to remember, commemorate, articulate, celebrate, etc., Bach? I trace an emotion, I trace a physical motion . . . every hour practicing in my youth . . . each prelude, each fugue . . . to learn is to imitate. At this moment (in life), imitating is not part of the solution. Instead I am developing a project of sound, which Bach (unknowingly) essentially canonized. This project of sound is not arbitrary. I am not obliged; it is a choice. Each step belongs to a tradition, although it will not further its development it nonetheless reveals a relationship . . .

Dorothea Baumann, in her systematic study of the relationship between music and space, provides an interesting point of departure. She differentiates between an interior and exterior spatiality of music, pointing out that:

> The spatial aspect of music has, in fact, two sides: music creates its own inner world with its own time, which is passing even if only in our imagination. A simple stream of sounds creates a sensation of space. But "musical" space is strangely ambiguous. Still, by means of thinking and sensation we can move within this virtual space, which has fullness and depth.
>
> (Baumann 2011: 65)

Baumann's approach acknowledges the significance of the inner spatiality of both sound and music, an aspect that is also relevant in Järnegard's conceptualization. David B. Knight introduces a different perspective in his reinterpretation of Murray Schaffer's concept of "soundscapes," one that resonates as well with some of Järnegard's ideas (Knight 2006: 3). Knight relates the notion of soundscape to that of landscape, claiming that it has two essential referential levels: one that is direct (description or quotation of landscape sounds) and one that is representational (reference to abstract and performance landscapes). His work explores these referential levels and their relationship to the composers' "geographies of the mind."[16]

My analytical hypothesis here, which unites Baumann's, Knight's, and Järnegard's readings, is that Bach had a specific conception of the physical sonic-dimension of his music, one that was necessarily related to the acoustic properties of the spaces where he performed throughout his life, the same spaces for which he wrote most of his music.[17] As I pointed out in the opening pages of Chapter 1, it took Bach seventeen years (1703 to 1720) to complete his Three Sonatas and Partitas for solo violin. During that period, the German composer worked in Weimar, Arnstadt, Mühlhausen, and Anhalt-Cothen, performing in spaces like Arnstad's Neue Kirche or the Mühlhausen Divi Blasii church. These spaces arguably shaped Bach's conception of sound, becoming part of the composer's "associated performance landscapes." It is within such reverberating spaces that a conception of violin polyphony as that conveyed in his BWV 1002 has been reimagined, reread, and transformed by Järnegard's vision.

> EJ: . . . as a composer I work with sound. I engage with sound through my body, the instrument, the space . . . I grab the instrument, beat and caress it, make it resonate. When I retract, I return to the desk and sound becomes an imaginative sign, a sign desperate to become a "reality" . . .

I do not claim that a conception of sound necessarily emerged from Bach's conscious act of intellectual reflection but that it is nonetheless critically significant, even if it remained at a completely unconscious level. A modern performer's approach to the music of the German composer might be dramatically transformed by a consideration of this "hidden" aspect. This perspective expands music's textuality once again to include the apparently un-notatable aspect of sound, understood as "sounding," as action/movement, and as resonating space. A trace that is nonsemiotic, that is, not linked to a sign, connects Bach and Järnegard, the process of dissemination escaping here the dimension of the written. This gesture parallels Derrida's discussion of communication, which – understood as a vehicle of meaning – must designate nonsemantic movement:

> this nonsemantic sense of the word communication . . . in one of the several so-called natural languages, constitutes the proper or primitive meaning, and that consequently the semantic, semiotic, or linguistic meaning [conveyed here in the score] corresponds to a derivation, an extension or a reduction, or a metaphoric displacement.
>
> (Derrida 1986b: 309)

EJ: . . . man is oriented against the world. Through movement we perceive reality. Through touch, through a slight movement of the elbow – the flickering gaze of the eye . . . however, movement is always accompanied by an inner reflection, preceding or proceeding perception . . . without movement, the world is silent, music illustrates this point . . . the body is not only a medium, but the creator. It is the body that ultimately can form and communicate what the mind can only imagine . . . the body extends where language ceases to suffice . . .

A simple look at the opening page of Järnegard's *double* will clarify some of my arguments (see Example 4.15 and Video 13). The first striking element is the division of the music into four separate parts, symbolically representing each of the four strings that resonate in Bach's original polyphony. The top part is performed live while the others are prerecorded and played on loudspeakers, which become mirrors of the performer's presence, specifically located around the audience. Sound has been torn apart, opened, and the audience has been invited to inhabit its inner space (see Example 4.16). A second striking element is the nature of sound, which moves amid nuanced indications that range between one and five pianos and sudden sound overloads, in gestures that seem to follow Luigi Nono's idiom in his final works like *La Lontananza Nostalgica Utopica Futura* (see Example 4.17 and Video 14). Sound has become a trace of sound that remains undefined, unclear, searching, nonassertive, as a residue, as "a signifier of loss of control."

DP: . . . my take, in perhaps a slightly different key than yours, is that the separability of the experience is the condition of the new taking up of the work because the music takes on a spatiality that is not controlled by the author – it is a gift, or a setting free of/into the work that makes the trace a signifier of loss of control, and not of mastery/power. Which is why it is not just establishing the condition for the possibility (or power) of a new work – like a new paradigm of frame that other works can also follow. It demands to be attentive to the impossible places – the spaces that cannot make a complete transformation into the space that is shared, etc. The difficulty, in other words, is the place where the trace is not simply spatiality/iterability, but where the impossibility of freedom by separating is performed as the task of responding to the music . . .

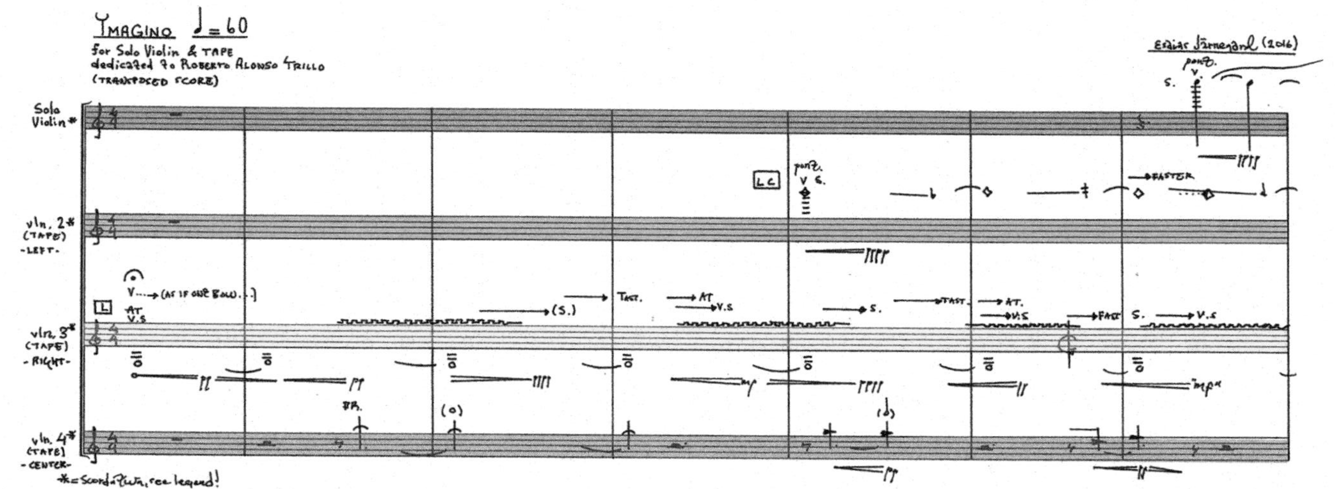

Example 4.15 E. Järnegard, *Ymagino*, opening measures

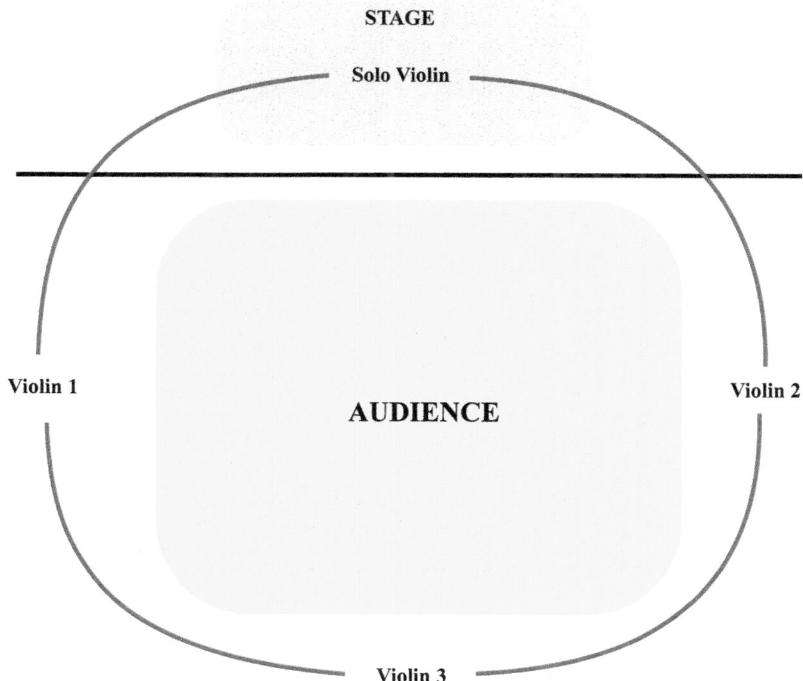

Example 4.16 E. Järnegard, *Ymagino*, stage disposition

> EJ: . . . each voice belongs to or begins in Bach. Bach's sound (memory) in the church, resonating, fading away. The reminiscence of the space, its sounding residue . . . the voices are parts of a whole, their counterpoint persists as an outstretched autonomy that becomes less and less apparent. Instead, it lingers as residue and memory in both its sound and construction . . .

Bach is thus brought back to life through traces that reflect on his otherness. Järnegard's music inhabits the inner spatiality of Bach's sound world but explores non-Bachian elements in an inversely affirmative gesture, Bach being asserted through his negation and *Ymagino* becoming a

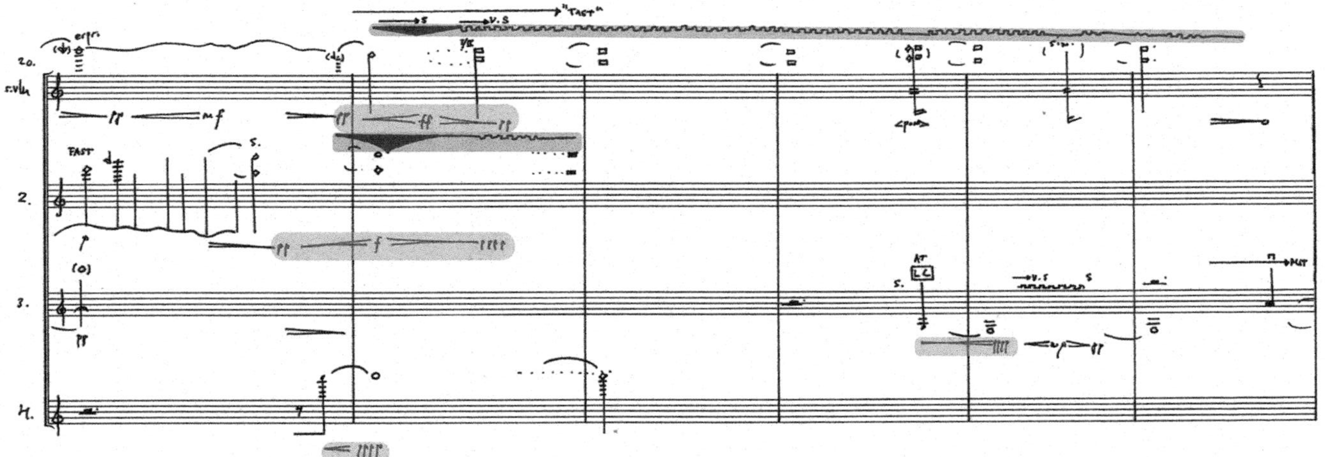

Example 4.17 E. Järnegard, *Ymagino*, mm. 20–25

"'representative of the outside' [that] is nonetheless constituted in the very heart of the inside" (Cobussen 2002: 83). The previous discussion of Derridean hauntology regains analytical transcendence here, Bach is affirmed through his absence, the very absence that grounds the possibility of a hauntological approach. If, according to Derrida, "to haunt does not mean to be present, and it is necessary to introduce haunting into the very construction of a concept," Järnegard creates a conceptual and experiential space in which Bach's ghost might join his hauntological game (Derrida 2006: 202).

Järnegard's music challenges as well the role of both noise and silence as music's framing elements, a challenge analogous to Richard Littlefield's discussion of the Derridean frame, and the traditional sound/silence opposition. The frame is internalized; silence and noise inhabit Järnegard's *Ymagino* and are consequently deprived of their role as music's otherness, as boundary-markers. Or perhaps they only reflect on the rigidity and counter-intuitiveness of a tacitly accepted assumption, they enunciate what music knows and musicological discourses ignore; they speak from music's inner space. Is the unheard gestural silence that fills the space between the notes in Bach's Tempo di Borea not one of its greatest performative challenges? Following Cobussen's reading of Cage's conceptualization of silence, we can claim that in *Ymagino*, as in Cage's *Waiting*, "a silence on silence opens. Silence is colored as a supplementary silence; it differs from itself" (Cobussen 2002: 127). Silence thus becomes what Cobussen terms *arche-silence*, silence as differentiation, not as an origin or as indifferent space but as "the non-sense of spacing, the place where nothing takes place but the place. But that place is everywhere" (Derrida 1981a: 257). *Ymagino* challenges the border between silence and its absence, Järnegard's music emerges at an undefined point, one that is only consciously assumed *post factum*, and it plays with endless shades of silence, thus embracing and deferring silence's circumscribing power.[18]

Transition

Let us now close the present argumentative circle by returning to the etymological consideration of *double* introduced in the earlier analysis of Matamoro's *(. . .)*. Marian Hobson employs Derrida's lexeme *pli*, the French term for "fold," to propose a different reading. According to Hobson, the suffix "-ble" (dou-*ble*) might originate from *plex*, the Latin version of *pli*. This lexeme plays a crucial role on Derrida's text on Mallarmé entitled the "Double Session" and on a section of his *Plato's Pharmacy* entitled "Play: From the Pharmakon to the Letter and from Blindness to the Supplement." In it, the French thinker argues that any repetition is dominated by a "strange duplication," one that combines a moment of truth and one of non-truth. This strange duplication, encapsulated in the word *double*, engenders the *eidos*, "the same, the clear, the stable, the identifiable in its equality with itself" while also allowing for the presence of what is to get lost, disperse itself, multiply itself "through mimemes, icons, phantasms, simulacra, etc."[19] The "fold" emphasizes the vision of meaning not only as an "ever-extending horizon of signification" but as structurally built "out of slippages and losses, out of graftings and cuttings" (Hobson 1998: 77). The previous analyses have endeavored to demonstrate this twofoldness by exploring the unstable-stability/stable-instability of musical artifacts through an expansion of the notion of musical textuality/text(i)ality (the *text*ual *text*ile). Furthermore, the analytical employment of authorship markers, emerging from the preceding discussion of Barthes's and Derrida's intellectual worlds, has showcased their power to introduce into the music-theoretical arena a novel approach to key aspects of the creative musical processes, to un"fold" and examine the creases of traditional musicological discourses and to question the work- and author-concepts posited by most transcendental analytic ontological approaches. These elements, explored here from the modest specificity that the . . . *Bach* . . . project – conceived as a game-of-doubles – represents, reflect nonetheless on the attributes of all Western classical music.

Notes

1 This chapter introduces a form of politextuality based on Derrida's model in *Glas*. My own writing is combined with small interpolations by Dr. Daniel Price (DP) and the composers Fernando Buide (FB), Miguel Matamoro (MM), Tomás Marco (TM), and Esaias Järnegard (EJ). This dialogic intertextual fabric raises unconscious connections while shaping the development of my own arguments as contestation and as part of that dialogic progress. The interpolations are intended to be disruptively enlightening, as a certain form of textual violence.

2 The term is also linked to mathematics and to the mathematical formula for remainders (*R*).

3 Derrida introduces such an examination of the fetish on a crucial reading of Marx's *Capital* in the final chapter of *Specters of Marx* (Derrida 2006: 156–222).

4 The full score of Buide's *Doble* can be requested from http://robertoalonsotrillo.com/portfolio-item/bachproject/

5 This example is taken from David Ledbetter's book *Unaccompanied Bach*. See Ledbetter (2009: 113).

6 A Midi version of Buide's original score was subjected to an *Aubio Pitch Detector* analysis in *Sonic Visualiser* and then exported and modified in *DataGraph*. Referential horizontal lines that represent the pitches of the G, D, A, and E strings are included to get an idea of register levels.

7 Derrida claims that all the conceptual oppositions of metaphysics:

> amount, at one moment of another, to a subordination of the movement of différance in favor of the presence of a value or a meaning supposedly

> antecedent to différance, more original than it, exceeding and governing it in the last analysis . . . "the transcendental signified."
>
> (Derrida 1981b: 29)

8 The full score of Matamoro's *(. . .)* can be requested from http://robertoalonsotrillo.com/portfolio-item/bachproject/

9 Derrida opens his 1972 book *Dissemination* with the following remark: "hence the necessity, today, of working out at every turn, with redoubled effort, the questions of the preservation of names: of *paleonymy*" (Derrida 1981a: 3).

10 A selection of significant recent contributions would include Leman (2007), Gibet *et al.* (2008), Gritten (2008), Gritten and King (2011), Larson (2012), Hatten (2014), Martinet *et al.* (2015), Cox (2016), McCaleb (2016), Leman (2016).

11 For a detailed discussion, see Lydia Goehr's "*Dopplebewegung*: The Musical Movement of Philosophy and the Philosophical Movement of Music" (Hermand and Richeter 2006: 19–63). For a broader discussion of the notion of *bewegung* and music, see Leonhardmair (2014).

12 The full score of Marco's *Double de Double* can be requested from http://robertoalonsotrillo.com/portfolio-item/bachproject/

13 In the Corrente, the chord underpins the opening arpeggiation.

14 The recording of Marco's *Double de Double* was subjected to an *Aubio Pitch Detector* analysis in *Sonic Visualiser* and then exported and modified in *DataGraph*. As in Chart 3.1, time in seconds is set against a vertical disposition of pitch, measured in hertz (Hz). Vertical areas marked in green show all the recurrences of Bach's signature chord.

15 The full score of Järnegard's *Ymagino* can be requested from http://robertoalonsotrillo.com/portfolio-item/bachproject/

16 This notion, coined by geographers David Lowenthal and Martyn J. Bowden, is linked to an exploration of the impact of environmental beliefs on human thought and action, that is, an examination of how our images of the world shape our relationship with it (Lowenthal and Bowden 1976).

17 A full list can be found in Leaver (2016: 142–191).

18 Connections with John Cage's ideas can be traced through a reading of Eric de Visscher's discussion of the three stages on the composer's developing notion of silence: from silence as a prerequisite for the introduction of sound, through a conception of silence as consisting of sounds, to a spatial conception in which silence is conceived as resounding in sounds (Visscher 1991: 48–52).

19 I believe that it is worth quoting the whole fragment:

> [T]here is no repetition possible without the graphics of supplementarity, which supplies, for the lack of a full unity, another unit that comes to relieve it, being enough the same and enough other so that it can replace by addition. Thus, on the one hand, repetition is that without which there would be no truth: the truth of being in the intelligible form of ideality discovers in the eidos that which can be repeated, being the same, the clear, the stable, the identifiable in its equality with itself. And only the eidos can give rise to repetition as anamnesis or maieutics, dialectics or didactics. Here repetition gives itself out to be a repetition of life. Tautology is life only going out of itself to come home to itself. Keeping close to itself through mneme, logos, and phone. But on the other hand, repetition is the very movement of non-truth: the presence of what is gets lost, disperses itself, multiplies itself through mimemes, icons, phantasms, simulacra, etc. Through phenomena,

> already. And this type of repetition is the possibility of becoming-perceptible-to-the-senses: nonideality. This is on the side of non-philosophy, bad memory, hypomnesia, writing. Here, tautology is life going out of itself beyond return. Death rehearsal. Unreserved spending. The irreducible excess, through the play of the supplement, of any self-intimacy of the living, the good, the true.
>
> (Derrida 1981a: 168)

References

Adorno, Theodor W. *Beethoven: The Philosophy of Music*. Cambridge: Polity Press, 1998.

Barnhart, Robert K., ed. *Chambers Dictionary of Etymology*. New York: Chambers Harrap Publishers, 1988.

Barthes, Roland. *The Pleasure of the Text*. New York: Hill & Wang, 1998.

Baumann, Dorothea. *Music and Space: A Systematic and Historical Investigation into the Impact of Architectural Acoustics on Performance Practice Followed by a Study of Handel's Messiah*. New York: Peter Lang, 2011.

Cobussen, Marcel. "Deconstruction in Music." PhD diss., Erasmus University Rotterdam, 2002.

Cox, Arnie. *Music and Embodied Cognition: Listening, Moving, Feeling, and Thinking*. Bloomington: Indiana University Press, 2016.

Derrida, Jacques. *Dissemination*. Chicago: University of Chicago Press, 1981a.

———. *Positions*. Chicago: University of Chicago Press, 1981b.

———. *Glas*. Lincoln: University of Nebraska Press, 1986a.

———. *Margins of Philosophy*. Chicago: University of Chicago Press, 1986b.

———. *Limited Inc*. Evanston, IL: Northwestern University Press, 1988.

———. *Specters of Marx: The State of the Debt, the Work of the Mourning and the New International*. New York: Routledge, 2006.

Freud, Sigmund. *Beyond the Pleasure Principle*. New York: W. W. Norton & Company, 1990.

Gallop, Jane. *The Deaths of the Author: Reading and Writing in Time*. London: Duke University Press, 2011.

Gibet, Sylvie, Nicolas Courty, and Jean-Francois Kamo, eds. *Gesture in Human–Computer Interaction and Simulation*. Marseille: Springer, 2008.

Gritten, Anthony, and Elaine King, eds. *Music and Gesture*. Burlington: Ashgate, 2008.

———. *New Perspectives on Music and Gesture*. Burlington: Ashgate, 2011.

Hatten, Robert S. *Interpreting Musical Gestures, Topics, and Tropes: Mozart, Beethoven, Schubert*. Bloomington: Indiana University Press, 2014.

Hermand, Jost, and Gerhard Richeter, eds. *Sound Figures of Modernity: German Music and Philosophy*. Madison: University of Wisconsin Press, 2006.

Hobson, Marian. *Jacques Derrida: Opening Lines*. New York: Routledge, 1998.

Knight, David B. *Landscapes in Music: Space, Place, and Time in the World's Great Music*. New York: Rowman & Littlefield Publishers, 2006.

Larson, Steve. *Musical Forces*. Bloomington: Indiana University Press, 2012.

Leaver, Robin A., ed. *The Routledge Research Companion to Johann Sebastian Bach*. New York: Routledge, 2016.

Ledbetter, David. *Unaccompanied Bach: Performing the Solo Works*. New Haven: Yale University Press, 2009.

Leman, Marc. *Embodied Music Cognition and Mediation Technology*. Cambridge, MA: MIT Press, 2007.

———. *The Expressive Moment: How Interaction (with Music) Shapes Human Empowerment*. Cambridge, MA: MIT Press, 2016.

Leman, Marc, and Rolf Inge Godøy, eds. *Musical Gestures: Sound, Movement, and Meaning*. New York: Routledge, 2010.

Leonhardmair, Teresa. *Bewegung in der Musik: Eine transdisziplinäre Perspektive auf ein musikimmanentes Phänomen*. Bielefeld, Germany: Transkript Verlag, 2014.

Lowenthal, David, and Martyn J. Bowden. *Geographies of the Mind: Essays in Historical Geosophy in Honor of John Kirtland Wright*. New York: Oxford University Press, 1976.

Martinet, Richard-Kronland, Mitsuko Aramaki, and Sølvi Stad, eds. *Music, Mind, and Embodiment*. Marseille: Springer, 2015.

McCaleb, J. Murphy. *Embodied Knowledge in Ensemble Performance*. New York: Routledge, 2016.

Price, Daniel M. *Touching Difficulty: Sacred from Plato to Derrida*. Aurora, CO: Davies Group Publishers, 2009.

Visscher, Eric de. "So etwas wie Stille gibt nicht. John Cages Poetik der Stille." *Music-Texte. Zeitschrift für neue Mursik* 40/41 (1991): 48–54.

~~Conclusion~~

> All these doors have a single lock and there is only one little opening into which the key can be introduced, and that spot is indicated only by the trace of the key.
>
> (Derrida 1981: 298)

After the preceding textual journey, it might seem paradoxical to even posit the true possibility of reaching and writing a conclusion. Engrossed in our present line of argument, we might claim that no text or music might sever the continuity of its ongoingness. I will nonetheless attempt to parallel a conclusive gesture by letting the text reflect upon itself, exploring its weaknesses and expanding the reflections included in the final lines of the book's introduction before I return to the opening questions and round off my overall argument with an examination of the significance that performance, understood as part of music's extended textuality, has had both in this text and on the . . . *Bach* . . . project.

Self-reflection

In an article entitled "Disciplining Deconstruction (For Music Analysis)" (Krims 1998) and originally published in 1998, Adam Krims introduced a valuable critique of the diverse musicological adaptations of Derrida's "deconstruction" that had been made up to that date. Following Krims, this section subjects my own text to those assessments in an attempt to explain and expose in an openly self-critical gesture how have I endeavored to counter (or not) the shortcomings found in previous related scholarship. Krims's first remark is made against the excessive reliance on Derrida's early writings and the overt simplification of his thinking.[1] A similar argument might be raised against this book, but how would it be possible to condense and thus unavoidably simplify Barthes's and Derrida's conceptualities without affecting the intricacy and unique fluid nature of their style? How can the various background historical sections sketched here not fail to fully convey the complexity of the processes that they endeavor to portray? One needs to modestly admit that in most cases, as Seán Burke remarks, the best commentary on Barthes and Derrida's texts is their actual reproduction: their work belongs to "that class of writing that precludes any sort of faithful summary" (Burke 1992: 47).

Krims finds fault as well with the "attempt at evocative language, the echoes of the writing style that often characterized early postructuralist" thinking, in the form of misreadings with particularly disciplinary motivations (Krims 1998: 301). What has the disciplinary motivation of the . . . *Bach* . . . project been? What is its hierarchical structuring? Has the musical been filtered through the literary, or is the literary the actual starting point and music a secondary reflection? Even if we accept the inescapability of the hermeneutic circle, I somewhat naively answer univocally and openly accept and embrace the partiality of my music-centered approach. Furthermore, the apparent uniqueness of my analytical perspective is denied by the fact that it exposes the very nature of any musicological enterprise since, following Kevin Korsyn's argument, "rather than worry[ing] about the purity of the field . . . we ought to recognize that music is always already postdisciplinary; it forms its objects with the aid of other disciplines, which are themselves in flux" (Korsyn 2003: 42).

Krims stresses that one of the central difficulties in engaging post-structuralist thought with music analysis is that its practice "seems to encourage us to essentialize analytical 'tools,' while postructuralist thought tends to militate against methodological closure" (Krims 1998: 305). I would argue that the analytical tools introduced in the previous chapter explore commonalities that eschew any sort of essentialism or methodologically closed structuring. I have attempted to avoid adopting Barthesian and Derridean notions in such a way that the "force of music-analytical discipline converts . . . [them] to an uncritical bottom line," an effort being made to use them not as a "result of music analysis but as a means of problematizing the very act and situation of music analysis," its methodologies and conceptual frameworks (Ibid.: 308 and 318).

In summary, this document can be self-reflectively defined against Krims's critical reading as a fabric of many unfinished parasitically related texts within a larger ongoing one, one in which tangential discursive paths necessary to develop the overall argument are taken, remain partially under-explored, and are eventually abandoned. But is that not always the case? This text lives in the awareness of that fact that it could have been otherwise. The choices made here, at all levels (musicological, analytical, structural, etc.), point towards an infinite otherness of approaches that do not counter but supplement this one. The music of the . . . *Bach* . . . project, its performance, and its conception have offered a certain level of resistance to the intellectual framework articulated here. These points of friction are the scars of a textual tissue that is unable to terminate, to come to an end, thus delineating the beginning of its still unwritten continuation. Fertile research that engenders new research, a chain of questions that might not have a definite answer but that need to be raised unremittingly anew.

Ritornello III

We can now finally return to the three critical questions drafted at the end of Chapter 1: how does the analytical perspective introduced in the previous chapter affect those opening hypotheses?

Should we consider the . . . Bach *. . . project as a single work?*

In the second Ritornello, I argued that the "dominant" modern work-concept could not be applied to the renewed understanding of musical textuality posited here. I also pointed out that the historical analysis of the emergence of its modern usage, introduced by Goehr, and its adaptation to musical discourses might make us question its pertinence within contemporary musicology without "yielding too much to the weight of . . . [its] accumulated intellectual and cultural baggage" (Perkins 2004: 40). The analyses presented in the previous section focused on aspects of music's extended textuality that, when examined under Barthesian and Derridean lenses, reinforce these arguments.

Barthes's article "From Work to Text" provides some enlightening insights that strengthen my line of reasoning. The French thinker points out that "against the traditional notion of the *work*, for long – and still – conceived of in a, so to speak, Newtonian way, there is now the requirement of a new object, obtained by the sliding or overturning of former categories. That object is the *Text*" (Barthes 1977: 156).[2] Barthes explains that the "work" can be understood as a corpus located in the methodological field represented by the Text and that, as a result, the Text should not be seen as the "decomposition of the work . . . [since] it is the work that is the imaginary tail of the Text" (Ibid.: 157). The Barthesian *Text* thus undermines traditional classifications through two critical features. On the one hand, it is radically symbolic – "a work conceived, perceived, and received in its integrally symbolic nature is a text " – and, on the other, it is irreducibly plural – "the intertextual in which every text is held, it itself being the text in-between of another text" (Ibid.: 159 and 161). "Network" and "fabric" become here the metaphors of the textual.

Derrida critically adopts Barthes's reading and its associated conceptual framework to introduce a vision of the text as a meaning-pregnant web of traces that lacks a genesis, arguing:

> The text is not conceivable in an originary or modified form of presence. The unconscious text is already a weave of pure traces, differences, in which meaning and force are united – a text nowhere present, consisting of archives which are *always already* transcriptions. Originary prints. Everything begins with reproduction. Always already: repositories of a meaning which was never present, whose signified presence is always reconstituted by deferral, *nachträglich*, belatedly, *supplementarily*.
>
> (Derrida 1978: 211)

In *Limited Inc*, Derrida proposes, from a slightly different perspective, a complementary understanding that illuminates as well my vision of musical textuality:

> The concept of the text I propose is limited neither to the graphic, nor to the book, nor even to discourse, and even less to the semantic, representational, symbolic, ideal, or ideological sphere. What I call "text" implies all the structures called "real", "economic", "historical", "socio-institutional", in short: all possible referents. Another way of recalling once again that "there is nothing outside the text" . . . It does mean that every referent and all reality has the structure of a differential trace.
>
> (Derrida 1988: 148)

The question remains: could such a fluid notion of the text and textuality be applied to music? *A priori*, as I pointed out elsewhere, musical and literary texts seem to be clearly distinct entities. But what happens when we expand our understanding of the textual following the Barthesian and Derridean models explored in the previous analyses? Let us consider the etymology of "text" and the historical evolution of its usage, its *paleonymy* (Derrida 1986: 329). According to the American Linguist John Lawler, in its primitive form, *teks* was a Proto-Indo-European idiom that meant to weave and to fabricate.[3] Through the addition of a suffix, it developed three distinct forms: *teks-la* came to mean web, net, or fabric; *teks-on* referred to a weaver, builder, or carpenter; and *teks-na* (the origin of the Greek *tekhne* and the Latin-based technique and technology) meant art, craft, skill. Furthermore, with an added prefix – *sub-teks-la* (subtle) – the term meant thin, fine, precise (Watkins 2011: 92). This *paleonymy* reveals that "text" has a historically charged meaning-scope, with potential musical connotations, that transcends its current literary-related treatment. Both "text" and "textual" thus become adequate terms to bridge the chasm that has emerged between the different and seemingly isolated dimensions of music as composition, performance, reception, and musicology. It is in the framework of this new musical textuality, or shall we say text(i)ality (the textual textile), that the *doubles* of the . . . *Bach* . . . project can be seen as oblique incisions across a Derridean *hymen*, a double-hinge that separates-yet-connects musical expressions of *oratio obliqua* and *oratio directa*, indirect and direct forms of speech/music.[4] That is, musical textuality as *dissémination*, *trace*, *restance*. These *doubles* and Bach's music engage in a process of mutual contamination to engender, following Cobussen, "a (partial) contact, but no (complete) assimilation. Both fusion and separation, and neither fusion nor separation; (n)either inner (n)or outer" (Cobussen 2002: 83). The resultant text is thus marked by its transversability, by its liminal nature, since:

> [i]t cuts across the circle from the place marked by Art on both sides. It is a line, a diameter of the circle. The text is not in the place of the artist nor in that of the artwork. The text is not produced – as such – by the artist, nor is it the product – as such – of an artistic production. The text is not unrelated to the productive activity of the artist nor to the createdness of the work. Yet it is also not identical with either . . . The text is the in-between of the artwork and the artist.
>
> (Silverman 1994: 54)

A renewed understanding of textuality that envisions the multiple dimensions of the "musical" as fluid, shifting, and organic is not compatible with the modern notion of the musical work articulated by most ontological readings, readings that seem instead to subject music to an interpretive intellectual autopsy. These approaches restrict the life of the analyzed body, sedating, and limiting the dynamism of the "musical" to accommodate their theoretic-analytical paradigms, music becoming an almost inert/dead entity. As Marcel Cobussen points out:

> The music text is off-center, located where the intra-musical meets the extra-musical, and de-defines its borders. Its textuality is the condition of not setting clear lines of demarcation between the inset and the outside of music, between what counts as part of the musical text and what does not.
>
> (Cobussen 2002: 23)

Is an alternative to the work-concept necessary? This book has attempted to show that it is not: music philosophy and music analysis might be approached in its absence by thinking outside the musical-work-box, by conceiving music beyond its objectual crystallization.

Who would the author of the . . . Bach *. . . project be? Is there one? Is there any?*

The previous analyses have showcased how the . . . *Bach* . . . project contests Romantic authorial individualism. The musical material, in the form of the explored traces or authorship markers, horizontally transverses vertically defined identities. Such an approach interweaves the weft of Lévinas and Derrida's "same" or "ego" – individual craft – into the weblike fabric of musical composition and musical textuality, an otherness where authorial subjectivities are contaminated.[5] From that perspective, musical authorship can be seen as a form of coauthorship, as an intersubjective or even collective enterprise.[6] Barthes reinforces this approach when he argues that the author might only return to the text as a guest, since "the I who writes the text . . . is never more than a paper-I" (Barthes 1977: 161). Such an idea can also be linked to Lévinas's consideration of trace in "The Trace of the Other." If creation, the relationship between the author and his work, is understood as a one-way-action, as a path of no return, then it is:

> possible only in patience, which, pushed to the limit, means for the agent to renounce being the contemporary of its outcome, to act without entering the promised land. The future for which the work is undertaken must be posited from the start as indifferent to my death. A work . . . is being-for-beyond-my-death.
>
> (Lévinas in Taylor 1986: 349)

Creation is thus envisioned not as a simple act of transcendence, one that implies an indifference to the finitude of the tangible and corporeal, but as a selfless movement toward the other. However, since the self is unavoidably inhabited by that same otherness, even in its idealized isolation, it remains articulated as a collaborative milieu, an inescapable multiplicity overtly exposed in the . . . *Bach* . . . project through a gesture that presents it as a gift.

Furthermore, in the game-of-doubles that the . . . *Bach* . . . project represents, the open exploration of mimicry, the mirroring of previous texts and compositional gestures, plays a crucial role that reveals often ignored but fundamental aspects of musical authorship. This is not an exception: all authorship involves an element of imitation tied to the "strange duplication" that permeates repetition, a duplication that, as discussed in the closing section of Chapter 3, engenders both the *eidos* (same, identical) and allows for the presence of what is to disperse itself in the form of *mimemes* (the ancient

Greek term for "imitated thing"). The resultant author/mime, according to Derrida, is both written and writing since "as soon as a mirror is interposed in some way, the simple opposition between activity and passivity, between production and the product, or between all concepts in -er and all concepts in -ed (signifier/signified, imitator/imitated, structure/structured, etc.) becomes impracticable" (Derrida 1981: 224). Authorial subjectivity needs to be consequently reconsidered, it stops emerging from writing to become the place of writing. Such a vision of authorship follows Derrida's discussion of writing and the textual, among an examination of the ideas of the French philosopher Jean Hyppolite, as a "subjectless transcendental field," one out of which the subject/author might be constituted.[7] But the field's function is not given, it is not an apriorism: it requires the gesture of writing/weaving in order to bear its becoming forward in time. That field becomes, in the . . . *Bach* . . . project, musical text(i)ality. In this light, the . . . *Bach* . . . project can be seen as an "author"-less enterprise, one that presents instead a text(i)al fabric in which intra- and intersubjective dialogues take place, creation/mediation happening within and being enabled by the textual space.

How can these questions help us contest the dominant notion of musical authorship?

The understanding of musical textuality that emerges from the perspective developed in this text leads to an understanding of music as a human intellectualization of sound (or archi-silence/archi-sound). This process is rooted in and emerges from a sublimation of basic elements linked to our perception of both selfness and otherness. Musical text(i)ality, as a result, can be seen as an endlessly ongoing process, linked to our very conditions of existence. In this light, creation takes place within an unfolding process of dissemination that precedes and follows it, a system pregnant with traces and traces-of-traces that iterate but that endlessly attempt to escape from and react to each other, in an expansive gesture of difference-differing-deferral. A composer does not simply work with sounds or with historically charged material, she/he works with(in) the fabric of musical textuality.

Coda – (performing) the . . . *Bach* . . . project (as performance)

The centrality of the performative dimension of the . . . *Bach* . . . project has been stressed elsewhere. I have pointed out that the project aims to rearticulate our traditional conception of performance, which becomes here a self-explanatory musicological activity. Furthermore, performance itself, the interpretation of both Bach's original material and of the new *doubles*, has had a reciprocal impact on the project's conception and on development of the arguments introduced in this book. Performance has also influenced the "universalist" aura of my approach, an approach that, while taking Bach's BWV 1002 as a case study, aims to reevaluate our understanding of authorship and workhood in a manner that transcends the historicist readings.

The conceptions of authorship and workhood sketched here stems from what I would define as the interpreter's inner performative view of music.[8] They emerge as a challenge to the current dominant institutionalized approach that leads to a vision of performance as the repetition of a historically bound repertoire under a single or usually limited musicological lens, a vision that, while taken for granted, has its roots in a set of aesthetic and performative traditions that can be tracked back to the nineteenth and early twentieth centuries. The challenge's pressingness becomes evident to any performer who stretches her/his repertoire to encompass early music and that composed in the present: she/he comes to realize that the relationship between the text/score, composer, and performance has had a historically fluid nature and that the role of the text, of the score as a mnemonic device, needs to be expanded if we are to advocate a novel and more malleable conception of our musical practices linked to the renewed understanding of musical tex(i)tality.

The recordings included in this book are as "textual," as musicological, as the written words are. Performing the . . . *Bach* . . . project places the interpreter in a space in which the book's main arguments are not only meaningful but coalesce in a tellingly enlightening manner. The project breaks the standard performative and reception expectations by expanding Bach's material, but, in doing so, it also demonstrates that nothing has changed: those paradigms were not betrayed by the novelty of the musical expansions but by the rigid edifice on which they were originally built. The player establishes a dialogue with the composers that is not individual, a plural conversation, a form of heteroglossia, a dialogue that is marked by its processual nature through gestures that are at once prospective and retrospective. Composition and performance become here a form of analytical commentary, two different forms of thinking (with)in music.

But why? How did we get this far? Because I am, in essence, a performer and performance shapes my understanding of music. The new approach to musical textuality explored thus far places performance inside the musicological domain; the margins are consequently shifted: "by means of the essentially incomplete nature of the unaccompanied solo pieces, Bach forces the listener and the performer to join the dialogue," a dialogue that is reflectively examined and expanded by the . . . *Bach* . . . project (Lutterman 2006: 42). As a result, the performance(s) included here become(s) the ultimate self-explanatory act of musical enlightenment, countering the vision of the composer, the score, or the work as teleological *causae prima*. As Derrida once wrote:

> This apparatus [music as performance] explains itself. Its self-explanatoriness does not imply, however, that one can explain it, that it can be comprehended by an outside observer: rather, it itself explains itself and already comprehends any observer. . . . It becomes more explicit as it multiplies, "*folding and unfolding the roots of its slightest signs*."
>
> (Derrida 1981: 299)

Notes

1 Krims pays special attention to Jonathan Culler's work, one of the secondary sources considered in the preparation of this text (Culler 1982).

2 The vision of the text as an "open sea" liberated from the author is seen by Barthes as a shift between a Newtonian and an Einsteinian model of the "literary" universe.

3 See Professor John Lawler's *Language Fossils* on http://www-personal.umich.edu/~jlawler/LanguageFossils.pdf

See also Onions (1967), Barnhart (1999), and Watkins (2011).

4 In *Dissemination*, Derrida defines *hymen* in the following terms:

> the hymen, the confusion between the present and the nonpresent, along with all the indifferences it entails within the whole series of opposites (perception/nonperception, memory/image, memory/desire, etc.), produces the effect of a medium (a medium as element enveloping both terms at once; a medium located between the two terms). It is an operation that *both* shows confusion *between* opposites and stands *between* the opposites "at once."
>
> (Derrida 1981: 212)

5 Elyse Pineau introduces a similar argument in her article "Haunted by Ghosts: Collaborating with Absent Others" that might be used to explore the connection between Bach's music and the new *doubles* in the . . . *Bach* . . . project:

> [I]n my writing practice, my collaborative partners are ghostwriters, internalized others, generally others long dead and reincarnated in any narrative moment through my articulation of them, in absentia and without their consent. Yet . . . I still want to claim collaboration, even though mine is the only materiality to put pen to paper or to take body to stage.
>
> (Pineau 2012: 459)

6 An interesting discussion of the nature of collective authorship is introduced in Uidhir (2011). A further illuminating point that reflects on aspects linked to the dialogic nature of the . . . *Bach* . . . project is made on a collaborative scholarly textual experience entitled *How Writing Touches*: "a spiral of 'sense-(of self)-making' is triggered that may, when the encounter is genuine and the collaboration rich, give birth to new persons, like recombinant DNA, constituting intertextual identities who subsequently are stage in dialogic response" (Gale *et al.* 2012: 41).

7 Derrida writes:

> In connection with the general signification of the *Epochē*, Jean Hyppolite invokes the possibility of a "subjectless transcendental field," one in which "the conditions of subjectivity would appear and where the subject would be constituted starting from the transcendental field." Writing, as the place of absolutely permanent ideal objectivities and therefore of absolute Objectivity, certainly constitutes such a transcendental field. And likewise, to be sure, transcendental subjectivity can be fully announced and appear on the basis of this field or its possibility. Thus a subjectless transcendental field is one of the "conditions" of transcendental subjectivity.
>
> (Derrida 1989: 88)

8 Under the solidified façade of the score and the historical sources used by musicologists, the performer experiences music from the inside, as a living and unfolding activity.

References

Barnhart, Robert K., ed. *Chambers Dictionary of Etymology*. New York: Chambers Harrap Publishers, 1999.

Barthes, Roland. *Image-Music-Text*. New York: Hill & Wang, 1977.

Burke, Seán. *The Death and Return of the Author: Criticism and Subjectivity in Barthes, Foucault and Derrida*. Edinburgh: Edinburgh University Press, 1992.

Cobussen, Marcel. "Deconstruction in Music." PhD diss., Erasmus University Rotterdam, 2002.

Culler, Jonathan. *On Deconstruction: Theory and Criticism after Structuralism*. Ithaca, NY: Cornell University Press, 1982.

Derrida, Jacques. *Writing and Difference*. Chicago: University of Chicago Press, 1978.

———. *Dissemination*. Chicago: University of Chicago Press, 1981.

———. *Margins of Philosophy*. Chicago: University of Chicago Press, 1986.

———. *Limited Inc*. Evanston, IL: Northwestern University Press, 1988.

———. *Edmund Husserl's Origin of Geometry: An Introduction*. Lincoln: University of Nebraska Press, 1989.

Gale, Ken, Ronald Pelias, Larry Russell, Tami Spry, and Jonathan Wyatt. *How Writing Touches: An Intimate Scholarly Collaboration*. Newcastle upon Tyne, UK: Cambridge Scholars, 2012.

Korsyn, Kevin. *Decentering Music: A Critique of Contemporary Musical Research*. New York: Oxford University Press, 2003.

Krims, Adam. "Disciplining Deconstruction (For Music Analysis)." *19th-Century Music* 21, no. 3 (Spring 1998): 297–324.

Lutterman, John Kenneth. "Works in Progress: J. S. Bach's Suites for Solo Cello as Artifacts of Improvisatory Practices." PhD Diss., University of California, 2006.

Onions, Charles T., ed. *The Oxford Dictionary of English Etymology*. Oxford: Oxford University Press, 1967.

Perkins, Leeman L. "Concerning the Ontological Status of the Notated Musical Work in the Fifteenth and Sixteenth Centuries." *Current Musicology* 75 (Spring 2004): 40.

Pineau, Elyse. "Haunted by Ghosts: Collaborating with Absent Others." *International Review of Qualitative Research* 5, no. 4 (Winter 2012): 459–465.

Silverman, Hugh J. *Textualities: Between Hermeneutics and Deconstruction*. New York: Routledge, 1994.

Taylor, Mark C. *Deconstruction in Context: Literature and Philosophy*. Chicago: University of Chicago Press, 1986.

Uidhir, Christy Mag. "Minimal Authorship (of Sorts)." *Philosophical Studies: An International Journal for Philosophy in the Analytic Tradition* 154, no. 3 (July 2011): 373–387.

Watkins, Calvert, ed. *The American Heritage Dictionary of Indo-European Roots*. New York: Houghton Mifflin Harcourt, 2011.

Postscript

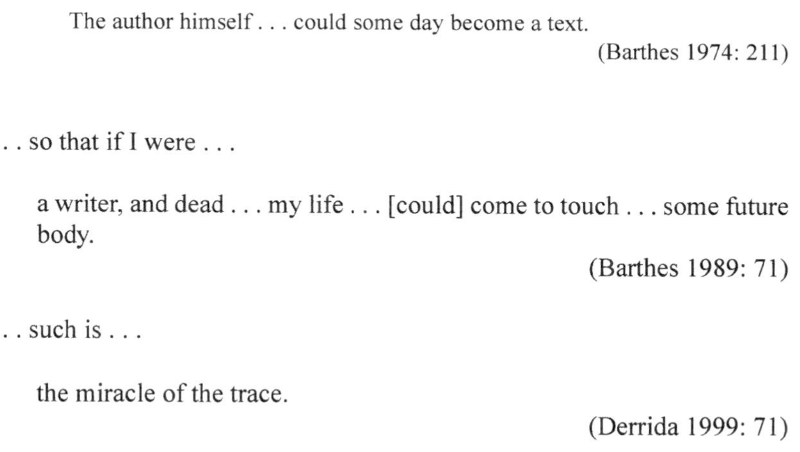

> The author himself . . . could some day become a text.
>
> (Barthes 1974: 211)

. . . so that if I were . . .

> a writer, and dead . . . my life . . . [could] come to touch . . . some future body.
>
> (Barthes 1989: 71)

. . . such is . . .

> the miracle of the trace.
>
> (Derrida 1999: 71)

References

Barthes, Roland. *S/Z*. New York: Hill & Wang, 1974.

———. *Sade, Fourier, Loyola*. Berkeley: University of California Press, 1989.

Derrida, Jacques. *Adieu to Emmanuel Levinas*. Stanford: Stanford University Press, 1999.

Annex

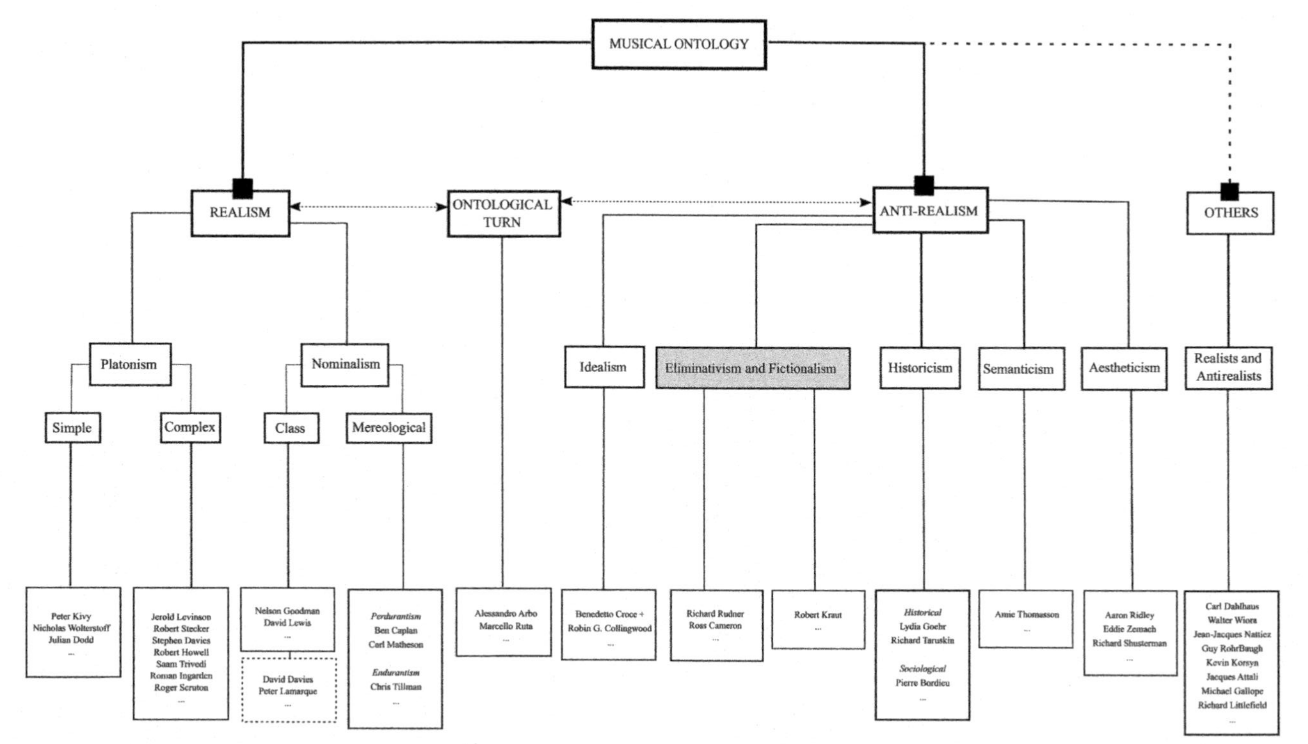
MUSICAL ONTOLOGY
REALISM
ONTOLOGICAL TURN
ANTI-REALISM
OTHERS
Platonism
Nominalism
Simple
Complex
Class
Mereological
Idealism
Eliminativism and Fictionalism
Historicism
Semanticism
Aestheticism
Realists and Antirealists
Peter Kivy
Nicholas Wolterstoff
Julian Dodd
...
Jerold Levinson
Robert Stecker
Stephen Davies
Robert Howell
Saam Trivedi
Roman Ingarden
Roger Scruton
...
Nelson Goodman
David Lewis
...
David Davies
Peter Lamarque
...
Perdurantism
Ben Caplan
Carl Matheson
Endurantism
Chris Tillman
...
Alessandro Arbo
Marcello Ruta
...
Benedetto Croce +
Robin G. Collingwood
...
Richard Rudner
Ross Cameron
...
Robert Kraut
...
Historical
Lydia Goehr
Richard Taruskin
Sociological
Pierre Bordieu
...
Amie Thomasson
...
Aaron Ridley
Eddie Zemach
Richard Shusterman
...
Carl Dahlhaus
Walter Wiora
Jean-Jacques Nattiez
Guy RohrBaugh
Kevin Korsyn
Jacques Attali
Michael Gallope
Richard Littlefield
...

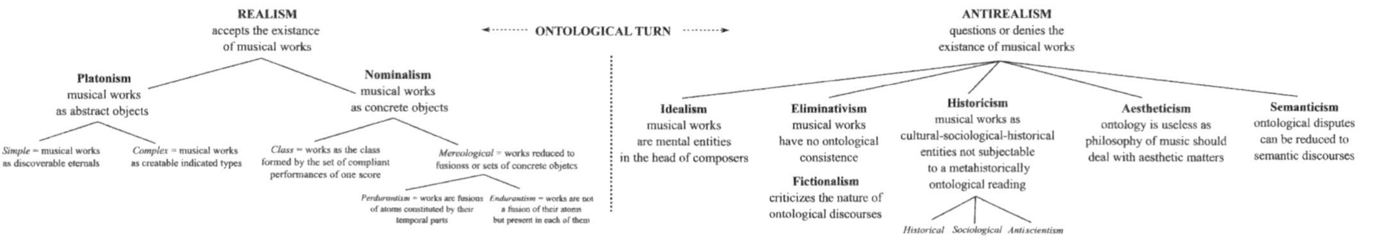

OBJECTIONS

Complex Platonist Objections	
Obscurity of the concept of indicated-type	Abstract entities are eternal even if the token of an indicated type exists only after the act of indication.
Sonicism versus Instrumentalism	Only the sonic and not the instrumental or performance-means dimension of a musical work should be considered as integral to its identity.
Works with identical identical structures	Two notationally identical works created by two different composers should be considerd as a single work.

Simple Platonist Objections	
The Perceptibility Objection	If Platonic entities are perceptually ungraspable, musical works cannot be Platonic entities.
The Creatability Objection	If musical works are created they cannot be abstract entities, which can only be discovered.
The Destructibility Objection	Musical works cannot be Platonic entities if we accept that they may be destroyed.

Nominalist Objections	
The Asymmetry Between Works and Performances Objection	Not all the properties of a musical work might be shared by a performance, and vice versa.
The Modal Objection	Contra the idea that a musical work cannot be identified with any particular sum or fusion of concrete manifestations
The Class Objection	Contra the idea of musical works as classes
The Ontological Economy Objection	In spite of ontological minimalism, classes are as ontologically unconvincing as abstract objects might be.

Figure 2.2 Different theories of musical ontology: definitions and objections

Table 2.1 Summary of literary authorship theories examined in Chapter 2

Phase	*Author*	*Key Ideas*	*Key Sources*
I Phenomenology, Formalism, and New Criticism	Edmund Husserl	Meaning/Intention dualism Objective meaning/Private intention	*Logical Investigations* (1900)
	William Wimsatt Monroe Beardsley	Intentional fallacy	*The Verbal Icon: Studies in the Meaning of Poetry* (1954)
II From the Death of the Author to the Re-Emergence of Intentionality	Roland Barthes	Impossibility of objective analysis Fluid meaning "Death of the Author"	*Writing Degree Zero* (1953) *S/Z* (1970) *Image-Music-Text* (1977)
	Jacques Derrida	Centrality of the reader Nonmonolithic reading of the text	*Voice and Phenomenon* (1967)
	Michel Foucault	Subject as culturally produced Contextualization Author-function Cultural regularities	"What Is an Author?" (1969)
	Wayne Booth	Understanding of intentionality as the path left by the author's choices	*The Rhetoric of Function* (1961)
	Elaine Showalter	*Gynocriticism*	"Toward a Feminist Poetics" (1979) "Feminist Criticism in the Wilderness" (1981)
	Luce Irigary, Hélène Cixous, and Julia Kristeva	*Écriture feminine* Femininity as constructed Author as performer of subjectivity	*The Sex Which Is Not One* (1977) *The Laugh of Medusa* (1975) *Desire in Language* (1969)

III Public Intentionality, the Text as Interpretation, and New Historicism	Elisabeth Anscombe	Public Intentionality	*Intention* (1957)
	Luigi Pareyson	Artistic intention as the outcome of interpretation	*Estetica* (1954)
	Umberto Eco	Openness Directive power of the author Analytical balancing of intentionality and nonintentionality	*The Open Work* (1962) *The Role of the Reader, Explorations in the Semiotics of Texts* (1976)
	Louis Montrose and Stephen Greenblatt	New Historicism Author's consciousness as historical and textual Socialized author	*Renaissance Self-Fashioning: From More to Shakespeare* (1980)

Table 2.2 Summary of the ontological considerations of the author- and work-concepts examined in Chapter 2

Type	*Author*	*Work/Author Definitions*	*Key Sources*	*Connections to Literary Theories*
Orthodox Realists	Nelson Goodman	Score as the work's only identity source Romantic author-concept	*Languages of Art* (1978)	Phenomenological intentionality
	Jerrold Levinson	Structural type of abstract object Traditional author-concept accepted as entrenched belief	"What a Musical Work Is" (1980) *Music, Art, and Metaphysics* (1990) *The Pleasure of Aesthetics* (1996) *Music in the Moment* (2007)	Foucauldian contextualism
	Peter Kivy	Simple Platonist approach Works are discovered rather than made Musical work *qua* idea	"Platonism in Music: Another Kind of Defense" (1983) *Authenticities* (1995) *Philosophies of Arts: An Essay in Differences* (1997)	Phenomenological intentionality
	Roman Ingarden	Work is purely intentional, immutable and permanent Score as foundation	*Ontology of the Work of Art: The Musical Work, the Picture, the Architectural Work, the Film* (1989)	Phenomenological intentionality
	Nicholas Wolterstoff	Music as a socially charged reality Necessity for an ontology of practices Music as an art of actions and not sounds	"Towards an Ontology of Art Works" (1975) *Works and Worlds of Art* (1980) *What Is Music? An Introduction to the Philosophy of Music* (1987)	Foucauldian contextualism
	Stephen Davies	Complex Platonism Works as universals versus performances as tokens	"The Ontology of Musical Works and the Authenticity of their Performances" (1991) *Musical Works & Performances* (2001) *Themes in the Philosophy of Music* (2003)	Foucauldian contextualism Eco's intentionality as cooperation

	Roger Scruton	Work as immaterial and intentional object of perception	*The Aesthetics of Music* (1997) *Understanding Music – Philosophy and Interpretation* (2009)	Phenomenological intentionality
	Julian Dodd	Works as eternal types Composer as discoverer rather than creator	"Musical Works as Eternal Types" (2000) *Works of Music: an Essay in Ontology* (2007)	
	Chris Tillman	Nominalist endurantism Atoms as concrete manifestations of the work The work is wholly present on each atom and thus multiply located	"Musical Materialism" (2011) "Musical Materialism and the Inheritance Problem" (2012)	
Unorthodox Realists	Carl Dahlhaus	Contests the traditional vision of the score Internalization of the analytical framework	*Systematische Musikwissenschaft* (1982) *Was Ist Musik?* (1985)	Foucaldian author-function New historicist authorship
	Peter Lamarque	Works have real and not ideal identities Works as cultural objects Identity conditions are value-laden, unlike those of functionally defined artifacts	"Work and Object" (2002) "On Bringing a Work into Existence" (2009) *Work and Object* (2010)	Pareyson's interpretative intentionality
	David Davies	"Action Theory" – Works of art are *actions*	*Art as Performance* (2004) "The Primacy of Practice in the Ontology of Art" (2009)	Derridean centrality of the reader Foucaldian author as a variable function of discourse

(*Continued*)

Table 2.2 (Continued)

Type	*Author*	*Work/Author Definitions*	*Key Sources*	*Connections to Literary Theories*
	Guy Rohrbaugh	Modal flexibility + Temporal flexibility + Temporality Against works as ideal structures	"Artworks as Historical Individuals" (2003) "I Could Have Done That" (2005) "Ontology of Art" in *Routledge Companion to Aesthetics* (2013)	Foucaldian author-concept
Ontological Turn	Alessandro Arbo, Marcello Ruta	Attempts to enable musicological research to deal with contemporary musical practices	*Ontologie Musicale: Perspectives et debats* (2014)	
Anti-Realists	Richard Rudner	Problematic abstractness of musical works Works as performances	"The Ontological Status of the Esthetic Object" (1950)	Barthesian centrality of the reader Pareyson's interpretative intentionality
	Lydia Goehr	Historicist perspective Work-concept as open, regulative, projective, and emergent	"Being True to the Work" (1989) "Writing Music History" (1992) *The Imaginary Museum of Musical Works* (2007)	Foucaldian focus on the emergence of the intentional and the textual Foucaldian contextualism
	Amie Thomasson	Semanticist perspective Meta-ontological critique of tacit ontological assumptions	*Fiction and Metaphysics* (1999) "Ontological Minimalism" (2001) "The Ontology of Art and Knowledge in Aesthetics" (2005)	Foucaldian author as cultural product New historicist textualized author
	Aaron Ridley	Negation of possibility and value of musical ontology	"Against Musical Ontology" (2003) *The Philosophy of Music: Theme and Variations* (2004)	Barthesian plurality

	Ross Cameron	Eliminativist perspective Composers create by letting pre-existing sound structures perform a role as musical works Problem of *epistemic access*	"There Are No Things That Are Musical Works" (2008) "How to Have a Radically Minimal Ontology" (2010) *The Moving Spotlight: An Essay on Time and Ontology* (2015)	Eco's openness and dual vision of authorial intentionality
	Robert Kraut	Meta-ontological critique Ontological discourses as attempts to justify already institutionalized intellectual practice	"Ontology: Music and Art" (2012) *Artworld Metaphysics* (2007)	
Alternative approaches	Jean-Jacques Nattiez	Semiotic approach Score as mnemonic device Music as "allographic" art Work as the combinations of a poietic strategy, a resultant trace, and an esthesic strategy	*Music and Discourse* (1987)	Barthesian multidimensional approach
	Richard Littlefield	Derridean reading Silence as frame	"The Silence of the Frames" (1996)	Jacques Derrida
	Michael Gallope	Deleuzian approach	"Is There a Deleuzian Musical Work?" (2008) "The Sound of Repeating Life: Metaphysics and Ethics in Gilles Deleuze's Philosophy of Music" (2010)	Gilles Deleuze

Index

Note: **Boldface** page references indicate tables. *Italic* references indicate figures and boxed text.